THE TIME OF YOUR LIFE

THE TIME
OF YOUR LIFE

16303

By

Donald L. Peters

RICHARDS ROSEN PRESS, INC.

New York, N.Y. 10010

The author and the publisher wish to express their appreciation to *Scouting* magazine for the use of material from the previously published article by the author, "Teen Fun Formula."

Published in 1975 by Richards Rosen Press, Inc.
29 East 21st Street, New York, N.Y. 10010

Copyright 1975 by Donald L. Peters

First Edition

Library of Congress Cataloging in Publication Data

Peters, Donald L.
    For the time of your life.

    1. Conduct of life. I. Title.
BJ1581.2.P47   170'.202   75–8970
ISBN 0–8239–0329–X

Manufactured in the United States of America

This book is dedicated to Clark Welch,
who first told me of his use of the
fun formula in counseling.

ABOUT THE AUTHOR

Donald L. Peters ("Leslie Peters" to the readers of his fiction) is a school counselor. He has traveled widely, talking with many teenagers and with the people who work with them in finding answers to their problems. He was the national president of the American School Counselor Association in 1970–71, served as a delegate to the White House Conference for Youth in 1971, and worked with many national committees, such as the ASCA committee on drug abuse concerns.

Don Peters has been working with teens since he was a teen himself. At fifteen he was holding a Scout troop together in the Mission District of San Francisco. At seventeen he was instructing classes in judo. At nineteen he was a paratrooper in France.

After World War II, he graduated Phi Kappa Phi, earned a master's degree in guidance and counseling, and, in the years since, has gained counseling experience at the junior-high, high-school, and college levels. He has shared experiences with teenagers that range from mountain climbing in the Grand Tetons to rap sessions in the Haight-Ashbury section of San Francisco.

His articles and fiction have appeared in *Good Housekeeping*,

McCall's Co-ed, Boy's Life, Ingenue, Real West, Family Circle, Woman's Day, American Girl, Scouting, and elsewhere, including magazines in Canada, Sweden, Scotland, Australia, South America, England, Denmark, and South Africa. This is his fourth book for Richards Rosen Press.

Mr. Peters lives in Montana with his wife (who he says, "does most of the typing and helps me spell all the big words in stuff like this") and two college-age sons. He is a counselor for the Billings public schools.

CONTENTS

INTRODUCTION

With no apologies for not solving quite all of the world's problems (I would if I could), this book is addressed to the vast majority of young people who would like to find more fun in life.

At the same time, I am not talking about the hollow stuff—the dumb kicks that go nowhere worth the trip, the miserable junk that turns off chances for more fun in the future, or the vicious regressions to the jungle that hurt good people and shut down the love cycle in our world.

This is a book for the people of now, who want to enjoy life, but more than only for the moment. It is for the people of both now and tomorrow, who favor the fun of building rather than the pathological glee of destruction, who want to experience life beyond the superficial, and who seek the adventure of making this a better world.

THE TIME OF YOUR LIFE

Chapter One

THE PURSUIT OF HAPPINESS

"I mean, I was lost, nowhere. No fun, no way." She sat cross-legged on the grass beneath eucalyptus trees in Golden Gate Park, a blond girl with tangled hair. "Now there's something. There's like highs and feelings. And there's me. I didn't know how beautiful I was, inside. I am a beautiful person, you know?" She ran spread, extended fingers up through her hair, then winced when she touched the purple bruise on her forehead.

Some of the kids around her laughed. A girl in a frayed Gypsy dress reassuringly squeezed her shoulders.

"Gloria is out of focus," said a dark-haired boy in a sweat shirt, "traveling distant lands. But that's what it is." His voice was slurred and hard to understand. "Self-discovery. Light where there was darkness. Gettin' it together."

"Bull," another broke in. "It's fun. Kicks. Just fun. And you don't have to say any more than that. With marijuana and acid, it's just trying to find a good time. And I don't see anything wrong with that."

"You would if you paid money for the crud I did last last week," said another voice. A mixture of groans and laughter followed.

"Or if you saw Gloria last night," said the girl in the Gypsy dress.

"But fun, man. That's where it's at," the boy in the sweat shirt again asserted.

"Well, maybe, to begin with."

"And after. Only different. We're all trying to feel better. And that's fun. Right? Anybody say that it ain't fun to feel better?"

"A little fun. A little happiness." Gloria was speaking, more to herself. "I'm entitled. Everybody has a right to fun."

Think of the brilliant rebels of the past who declared for us a creator-endowed, inalienable right to the pursuit of happiness. A wonderful heritage. And although the words did not make it to the Constitution, the Bill of Rights carried forward the intent and provides for specific rights which make this pursuit both possible and fruitful.

In essence, the main difference between the free Western countries, no matter how imperfect, and the totalitarian regimes may well be in the opportunities of people to have fun. On our side of the curtains, there is the chance. There is, without great fear and threat, the chance for fun and the good life. There is the right to the pursuit of happiness.

Of course, no one can guarantee you happiness. You have to work it out. And this is no simple thing. It has to be understood. A lot has to be understood, about a lot of things. There are a lot of misunderstandings, a lot of faulty ideas. Fun or the lack of it is tied to many things.

What Do You Mean, Fun?

Time out for a definition. What do we mean by fun? Much of this book is meant to help you round out your own set of functional definitions. If you disagree with the points of view and definitions suggested, no sweat. Chalk it up to mental exercise. Refine your own ideas, the way they make the most sense to you, the way you see them fitting into your own life situation and style. But we will recognize again and again that the word "fun" means different things to different people.

It would be easy to challenge the use of fun as a term to cover a vast and varied collection of feelings. The temptation is there, for example, to expound on the subtle differences between joy and happiness, or at least to demand a different category for ecstasy as distinguished from kicks.

Some things under the general heading of fun feelings are beautiful, rapturous delights with an intangible spark of eternity. At another extreme, there are those feelings experienced as temporary blasts of emotion that are destructive, disruptive, and painfully remembered with harsh regrets and shame.

We could get lost among multidimensional continua in searching out precise definitions and considering the shadings and connotations of an infinite number of physical and psychological satisfactions. Fun is, indeed, an oversimplification.

Do not set me up against the printed Webster's. But by fun, in this book, is meant the grand, wide spectrum of good times, in contrast to the bad. It is the stuff on the positive and pleasurable side of life, the stuff that normal, healthy people want more of.

Here, the meanings of fun are in the way *you* use them and the way we hear them used, commonly and uncommonly. For example:

"Hey, you guys have all the fun!"

"I hate to say we ought to break up, Charlie. But face it. We just aren't having fun together. We used to have fun. But not now."

"My folks don't let me have any fun. I can't do nothin'."

"We didn't mean to hurt him. And we sure didn't know the thing was loaded. We were just trying to have a little fun."

"Some guys don't like this kind of work. Me, I think it's kind of fun."

"Come on, Grace. Fun's fun. But lay off, will you?"

"And, George, just cut it out. That's no fun. I don't like that at all. You're just going to ruin everything. George!"

"Well, Mom, I told you I wasn't going to have any fun at that dumb party. And I was right."

Chapter Two

THE FUN FORMULA

While working with young people in the Mission District of San Francisco, we looked hard at what went right and what went wrong with a wide variety of activities, trying to discover criteria for successful events of all kinds. From our experience came what was termed the teen-fun formula. Revised and refined, it continues to be a valid, dependable guide for both planning and evaluation, not only of teen fun, but of adult fun as well. It can be of help when thinking of short-term events, long-range programs, and, most significantly, life.

Action

The thing we agreed should top the list is the word "do." Kids not doing anything weren't having any fun. And programs in which people were supposed to do nothing but be nice and sit on their hands were flops. It takes *action*, more times than not, in order to have fun.

Think of a boy, sitting on his front steps, staring at concrete on a Saturday morning. It is a nothing day. He shrugs, gets up from the steps, sets out for the park or the museum or to see who is at the Boy's Club, and already he feels better. Just getting into motion makes it more fun than it was.

But, as you know, it is no simple thing to get into motion. There is the problem of inertia. A tremendous push is often needed to get the action started, especially when you have been inactive for a considerable length of time. It may take the help of other people to get you going.

Slumps are easier to slip into than out of. So many things tend to minimize the *do*, the going action, in this modern world. The television, the movies, the radio, the automatic record changer, and the automobile all tantalize and entertain but minimize the need to *do* and really be a part of the action.

It is no wonder that so many people come to feel that they should magically be provided fun and happiness without effort, somewhat as a baby finds a ready nipple when he is hungry or a warm blanket spread over him when he is chilled. But those who find satisfying good times have come to understand that they must have an active part in their own entertainment.

Learning and Discovery

Another thing we observed when we were trying to analyze the components of fun was the fact that people perked up and joined in whenever there was something new to be learned.

Nothing catches on like *something new*, a new sound in music, a new dance step, a new skill, a new place to go. It might be a new idea, or it might be a new understanding of something so old that it can be new all over again—anything which offers challenge and brings that wonderful feeling that comes with success.

In spite of traditionally voiced dislike and resistance to schoolwork, people enjoy learning. It is a natural function of every normal, developing, healthy person.

In our early teens we were afraid of being laughed at, and of admitting that we were not as sophisticated and grown-up as we felt we should have been. We held back from asking questions about our most pressing concerns, sometimes because we lacked the courage, sometimes because we doubted that we would get a straight answer that would be worth the embarrassment of the asking. But the questions were there underneath, wanting and needing answers.

Now that we are more mature, we are still reluctant to ask as many questions as we might. Some of the old reasons are still there. But we also are better equipped to work out answers for ourselves. And personal, active discovery is more fun.

"What's new?" we say. A walk around town, a TV show, and a class are empty things when nothing new is learned, when no discoveries are made. But if the walk leads to a new friend, the TV plot works out in a new intriguing way, or the class turns up a practical answer to a personal question, and suddenly, it is fun.

Emotional Experiences

Another ingredient of a good time is the provision for emotional experiences. Parents, especially, tend to be protective and fearful when it comes to this area. They want to shelter the young and restrict them to calm havens.

But the drive toward excitement and emotional expression is there in all of us—young and old—demanding outlets. Though sternly suppressed in some, it is there. We could not survive or continue the species without it.

Who does not like to laugh, or sometimes cry, or to feel the tingle going up the spine during a sacred or patriotic moment? Even fear, the terrible, and the horrible are often fun, as long as all ends well. Both comedians and fictional fiends will always have their followings!

Exhilarating get-togethers include uproarious moments. Funny and exciting things happen. Sometimes they are impromptu and unexpected, sometimes they are prearranged and worked into the plans for a successful happening. The most enjoyable dances often take place in stimulating settings—sometimes with dim lights and shadows, sometimes with bright, pulsating, colored lights and ever-changing projected designs cast across the scene. Amplified music is often overwhelming.

It is natural for many people to hold back either because they are a trifle shy or because they are afraid to enter in. But eventually, they learn that the very best times are lasting, meaningful experiences, with a significant degree of emotional investment.

That Need to Belong

The most pathetic picture at any gathering is the outcast, the kid on the sidelines, who maybe sticks it out for a time, but finding no one wants to relate to him, slips away as inconspicuously as possible. "Who needs it? Not me," the defenses come in to say. But all of us need to feel that we belong.

Fun is impossible when we feel shunned and rejected by those around us. The hostess who neglects newcomers or does not make sure that everyone knows each other and that no one is left out of things has fallen short. The discussion leader who fails to guarantee that each member of the group has an opportunity to contribute has likewise fallen short. It is no fun to be left out. It can be a threatening and frightening experience.

This being the case, the small group pattern usually results in more fun than do the mob scenes. Even big school affairs break down into smaller groups. And those who are not included in these smaller groups may feel very much alone within the crowd.

Good times happen in the company of people who accept us. We are most likely to have fun with our family and friends, with the people we have shared our fun with in the past, and with people it will be shared with again in the future.

A Voice in What Is Going On

Another thing that has been more than obvious about teen fun is that teenagers like to feel they are doing their own thing. They do not like to think that everything is being done for them. They don't like to be pushed into doing things they don't want to do, things that somebody else thinks they ought to be doing. When adults take over too much and try to provide good times without the teens themselves having a part all the way, the fun falls short of what it might and should have been.

In order to have fun, teenagers need a reasonable voice in deciding what they are going to do. It makes sense that they should have a part in the selection of their activities and in the planning and work involved.

Being Somebody

You cannot have much fun if you lack significant, healthy identity. It is a sad and empty world when you do not feel you have a meaningful part in it. This is related to belonging to a group and it involves the need to be recognized as being important enough to have a voice in what goes on around you. But there is more.

Remember back in gym, in the park, or maybe on the street when the kids chose sides for softball or skin-the-cat? And remember the kid who was not chosen? Maybe you even had a turn at being that kid. This kid did not have much fun—unless some enlightened leader-type assigned him to be manager, first base coach, bat person, scorekeeper, umpire, or something.

Everybody has to be somebody. It is intolerable to hang out as a nobody. If a constructive role does not seem to be available, a destructive role is likely to come into play. When it does not seem possible to be a successful, contributing individual, then an inadequate, failing sponger or a violent militant is liable to evolve. Those refused as friends may be expected to become enemies.

If you think about it, the inevitable consequences are easy to see. When you force people out of it and refuse to help them be a part of your good times, certain dynamics come into play that can hinder everyone's fun.

The Ever Important Look Ahead

Another thing we finally focused on when analyzing good times, a few years ago in San Francisco, was the importance of always keeping something out front, ahead of where we were in time and space.

If you have to break, swing to the sign that reads, "Hey, more to come, right after . . ."

In a number of ways, it turns out that the concluding ingredient in the best of fun is tied to an intelligent recognition of the future.

Good times never end. Each one includes a look ahead to even better times.

For example, a girl comes home from a glorious date. There was action; they did things. There was learning and discovery; they did new things, things they had never done before. There was emotional experience; the music was exciting and, afterwards, the moon. There was an incomparable feeling of belonging; at times during the evening they experienced the most intense feelings of belonging they had ever known. And there was surely a voice in their own affairs; they had the deciding voice in what they did from the time they left until the time they returned. All of the first six ingredients for fun are there. But it takes one more. At this point the fun of the evening is still a fragile thing, indeed.

The boy brings the girl to her door. There may be a perfect goodnight kiss. But then, if one or the other indicates, "No more," just "See you around," thud.

If there are no expectations of more dates and even happier times ahead, then, suddenly, it is not fun anymore.

That which ends just is not any fun. For those who want to enjoy life, it is absolutely necessary to plan ahead and do things to sidestep those empty "What-now?" feelings. And there are worse feelings.

Consider the fun date one more time. Regardless of the thrills experienced, if the evening is plagued with feelings of guilt or fear of consequences, it falls short. Or, later on, if the evening's action results in serious regrets, if after the chemistry dies down they wish they had not done what they did, or if it becomes apparent that one really was not as serious and genuinely involved as the other supposed, then fun turns into bitter feelings at the opposite end of the scale.

Life is an on-going process, and the joys of living are forever linked with the need for an optimistic outlook for the future.

The Teen-Fun Formula

Almost any attempt to analyze and explain human behavior results in oversimplification. Trying to define what makes for a good time is no exception. There are uniquely individual, personal problems that can interfere with a person's capacity for having fun.

But I have learned that, even in the more complex situations, it can help to keep these seven points in mind. The fact is, when things are a bit on the complicated side it is especially important to apply a few rational concepts with which to think and to consider the situation point by point in terms that are understood by those involved.

When seeking fun as an individual or when planning group events, meetings, conventions, or anything where you want people to have a good time, your answers will be found in well-rounded activities that

1. Keep people in motion, physically and/or mentally.
2. Offer opportunities for discovery and learning.
3. Provide genuine emotional experience.
4. Foster a feeling of belonging.
5. Permit them to have a say in what they do.
6. Recognize them as significant somebodies.
7. Include the look ahead and lead toward happy, worthwhile things to come.

The formula works. Test it. Use it as a checklist in planning your good times. Use it as a follow-up in trying to figure out why things go wrong.

Through this book, we will be looking in greater depth at these several points of the fun formula, and then on into other related aspects of the fun things in life.

But first, in order to communicate on an in-depth level, it is imperative that we understand a few of the basic dynamics involved. If we are to understand what it takes for people to have fun, we have to have some understanding of people and why they act the way they do. The next four chapters are fundamental in consideration of the loaded subjects discussed later in the book.

Chapter Three

PSYCHOLOGY HELPS

During the opening session of the school year, when I teach psychology, I call to the front of the room a husky, good-natured young man and announce we are about to conduct our first psychological experiment. I tell the class that the point to be made is the most important in the entire course and will be repeated later on in many different ways. The concept to be illustrated is the foundation of understanding human relationships and human behavior.

I ask the boy to take a comfortable stance in front of the group and ask him to make no unnecessary movements. "If you feel you have to change the position of your feet or body," I tell him, "do what you feel you have to do. Hold your new position until you feel you have to change again."

Then I proceed to push him with well-spaced little shoves, from the side, front, and back.

First I shove with some force from the side. He does not change position. And I say, "See what a stable animal he is when pushed from this angle. This obviously is not his weakness. But look. . . ." I push his back with my little finger, and he totters and moves a leg forward to keep his balance.

After a few more pushes, enough to make the subject change his position a half dozen times, I mumble a pensive, "Isn't that interesting? I wonder why he didn't fall down?" I thank the boy for his cooperation and ask him to return to his seat.

Next, I go to the board and write the word "homeostasis" in big, bold letters.

"Homeostasis," I say, "is defined, for your notes, as *the tendency of the body to maintain balance*. A basic characteristic of all living beings is the predictable tendency to attempt to maintain balance in all ways. As to this informal experiment, the general response of the subject was absolutely predictable. We knew he would try to keep his balance. To be off-balance can be a threat to our very survival. When thrown off-balance in any way, we react immediately to regain balance.

"Once in this little experiment, the young man who was the subject did not understand he was permitted to move his legs. He fell all the way to the floor. But even in this case, he maintained balance, in his own way. He put out his hands and neatly cushioned his fall. He protected himself."

Then, after a brief pause, I say, "There is something else we knew would happen in this experiment, something not so obvious to an unthinking observer. He didn't like it. Sometime I'm going to shove somebody in this so-called experiment, and he is going to turn and bust me right in the mouth. Happily, today our subject was an intelligent gentleman who recognized it was all in the interests of science, and he let me get away with it. But whether our subject today chooses to admit it or not, we know he felt like pushing back. It is no fun to have to stand up in front of everyone and be pushed around. It is embarrassing enough to make a person downright angry."

Frustration-Aggression Cycle

Consistent with the principle of homeostasis, when we get pushed, we feel like pushing back. When we are thrown off-balance or blocked from having things the way we want them, we feel like striking back at the person who is to blame. This tendency is present in all of us. Frustration tends to result in aggression.

Frustration is the state of being off-balance and blocked from having things the way we want them. However, the unpleasant feeling that goes with the blocking of our motives is so closely linked to the blocking that the word "frustration" is often used to mean the feeling as well as the blocking.

Aggression may be defined as an act that is intended to cause injury and hurt. Aggression may be directed toward that which is blamed for the frustration or toward some substitute for that which is blamed.

Let me repeat, *frustration tends to result in aggression.*

Nick has been counting on going out with friends that Friday evening. At breakfast his father reminds him that this is the night Nick was going to have to help him do some painting. (Frustration.) Nick grumbles and slams the door as he leaves. (Aggression.) His father orders him back, makes him close the door more softly, and tells him, "Any more of that kind of stuff and you aren't going to be seeing those friends of yours for a month." (Frustration.)

On the way to school a boy bumps into him, and Nick hits him hard on the shoulder. (Aggression.) A moment later a much larger boy grabs Nick by the shirt front and tells him, "You ever touch my little brother again, and I'll pound you into the ground like a stake." (More frustration for Nick.)

In school he is standing when the bell rings. The teacher asks him to take his seat. He mumbles something under his breath. (Aggression.) "What was that you said?" the teacher asks him in front of the class. (Frustration.) He tells her, and more! (Aggression.) "Report to the Assistant Principal!" she orders. (Frustration.)

One more act of aggression, and Nick may be suspended from school. More acts of aggression after that, and there will be increasingly serious trouble.

As you can see, frustration not only tends to result in aggression, but also aggression tends to result in additional frustration. It is a cycle. Frustration leads to aggression; aggression leads to greater frustration; greater frustration leads to greater aggression, and in turn, to even greater frustration. There seems no end to it, at least no happy end.

When someone strikes out to offend and hurt another person, this aggression is frustrating to the other person, and he, too, may be expected to have the normal reaction of aggression, which he believes to be justified defense or revenge. Add to this the many rules and laws against aggression, and it is difficult to understand how anyone can suppose that bare aggression ever pays off.

Admittedly, there is an animalistic joy in lashing out and drawing blood in a moment of revenge. But the quick pain of retaliation, long-term punishment, and shame are the consequences. Control of our aggressive impulses is a logical price we must pay for civilized, group living.

Frustration in life is inescapable. The basic urge to be aggressive when we are frustrated is also inescapable. But it is not irresistible for normal, healthy, mature people.

Of course, we must recognize that there are many severely frustrated people in this world, people who are far from having things the way they want, people who are repeatedly blocked from reaching their goals. And as a consequence, there are many people who are constantly caught up in the cycle, who are hair-triggered and set to be destructively aggressive at the slightest additional frustration.

Failure to understand and cope with the frustration-aggression cycle contributes to much of the misery on earth. The problems of name-calling, prejudice, revenge, crime, war, and even lovers' quarrels have roots here. Minor problems fireball into catastrophies because of our lack of ability to arrest this vicious cycle. Things being as they are, we have continuing need for increased support for institutions and services that are designed to head off trouble and break the cycle in various aspects of life.

On the teen level, one of the best purposes I know for having professional counselors in every junior high and high school is to head off the needless trouble which can be caused by the frustration-aggression cycle. In a school with an adequate counseling staff, teens have a way out when they feel they are near exploding, a way of letting off steam without making their problems worse.

If teens have an understanding counselor and a confidential setting, they *talk out* their aggression instead of *acting out*. This breaks the cycle by preventing the additional frustration which results from open aggression. And incidentally, talking it out is more healthy than keeping the aggressive feelings bottled up inside. Continually keeping feelings bottled up can cause trouble and discomfort in other complex ways.

Size up the counselors in your school. Ask around and find out if they are people you can trust and open up to.

Our Personal Needs

When we know a person's needs, we can better understand why he acts the way he does. If we know a man has been out on the desert for two days without water, we can understand his impatience to have a drink. When we know a girl wants to go to college but her family does not have the money to send her, we can understand why she saves most of the money from her part-time job, instead of spending as freely as others in her crowd. When we know a boy has become interested in a new girl, we can understand why he has started being disagreeable around his steady.

We always have purposes for what we do, confused and complicated though they may be. And whether we admit it or not, *the reason we do what we do is to satisfy our own personal needs.* The fundamental urge to satisfy our needs is behind everything we do. This is true for the best of us and for the worst.

This makes us all sound selfish, doesn't it? And we are undeniably selfish—but not in the popular sense. We all look out for our own selfish interests. But the word "selfish" loses its usual connotation when we grasp the concept of *self.* For most of us, the self includes much more than a mere physical body and a collection of animalistic urges to keep us alive and functioning. However, we must also realize that there are some people so dominated by physiological and survival needs that they find it impossible to sense much beyond these needs.

The Hierarchy of Needs

To stress a point I sometimes tell a story about a boy who broke through the ice on the Yellowstone River one winter day. He was clinging there by his fingernails, trying to keep from being pulled under by the current, when a teacher passed by and heard his cries for help. This was a good teacher, and she could tell right away the boy had a problem. And she went out there on the ice to help. At considerable danger to herself, she went right out there and sat down at the edge of that broken ice beside him, and opened the textbook and assigned him Problems 93 through 104, at the close of Chapter 6. But wouldn't you know, he was one of those uncooperative kids. I mean, he hardly paid any attention or even tried. Like I said, this was a good teacher. She did not let it end there. She really wanted to help. And she had taken a couple of courses in guidance. She tried reasoning with him about how important this work was to his future.

This is only a story, but I have known too many people who talk as though school should be concerned only with teaching and not with the "personal life" of its students—as though the two could somehow be separated. I have always believed that when a girl becomes pregnant or a boy commits suicide, it interferes with their study habits. The school must be concerned with the student as an actual, whole person if it is to do a job worth doing.

To help us understand the nature of needs in ourselves and in others, the psychologist A. H. Maslow pointed out that needs are arranged in a hierarchy, ranging from the most urgent bodily needs to the higher, acquired, psychological needs. That is, there is a sequence in which our needs are felt or become known to us. Our more basic needs must be satisfied before we can sense, to any great extent, the existence of others higher up the scale.

The first level in this hierarchy is our need for air, water, food, and other *physiological* necessities. Next comes a need for *safety*. We all need a measure of security, but this comes after a relative satisfaction of our bodily needs. When we grow severely thirsty or hungry, we will risk our lives for water or food.

Next comes a need for *love*, attention, and belonging. Next, *esteem* or self-respect, prestige, and recognized success.

Highest in the hierarchy, according to Maslow, is *self-actualization* —that is, the need for self-fulfillment, for becoming the most that we are capable of becoming. The majority of our academic school subjects are related to this level.

Some cases do not fit neatly into this sequence, but the tendency toward such order is always present. And in dealing with any problem involving needs, the concept of the hierarchy of needs should be taken into account.

The boy in the icy river does not see much point in studying schoolwork until his basic safety needs are met. Schoolwork has no meaning for him until he is out of the water, warm and dry, and sure he is going to live. A love-starved girl from a rejecting home feels her need for affection more strongly than her need for self-respect and a pure reputation. The people of a country in dire need of food and the other necessities of life are not concerned with their right to a democratic system of government until their basic needs are met. They may be expected to support that system which appears to supply their immediate needs. Bodily and safety needs require satisfaction before most people sense a need for dignity, self-respect, and political freedom.

But as surely as the higher needs are not felt until the basic needs are met, the higher needs *will* be felt when the basic needs have been met. Once the boy is out of the river and knows he is safe and secure, he will see a need for schoolwork. Once the girl finds sufficient love, she will care more about her reputation and her self-respect. Tragically, she may discover too late that the love she wants is linked with her reputation and her self-respect. She may find that her frantic strivings for love have worked against her, giving her only temporary satisfaction and robbing her of the lasting love that she later discovers she needs most.

The people in dire need of the basic necessities will want much more of life once these are satisfied. They will come to want a higher standard of living, the self-respect and dignity that go with independence, and a voice in their own affairs.

There is a lesson here for those who sincerely want to help others, whether it be individuals helping other individuals or nations helping other nations. When we undertake to provide the basic necessities of life to people in need, we would be naive to think they will then be content. New needs will promptly be recognized.

The future is predictable in this respect. We should consider beforehand what may be the next need to arise and how it may be satisfied. Certainly, the helping person or nation should not be so childish as to expect continued expressions of gratitude—with the new need for self-respect, the people may not want to admit or even remember that they ever had such a need for help.

It becomes apparent, then, that the needs we humans feel are determined as much by what we have as by what we do not have. By answering the needs of people, we create new needs within them, needs which can no more be ignored than the original basic needs.

If you grasp this concept, congratulations. Unhappily, most people do not. And neither do they act in concert with the dynamics at work here.

Chapter Four

WHO ARE YOU, YOUR *SELF?*

Then, there's the girl who said, "Every place I go, I have to take myself along. And that ruins all the fun."

Who do you take along? Do you have an answer to the question, "Who am I?"

Many people are inclined to think of themselves as just that thing they see reflected in the mirror now and then, that fabulous collection of muscles and bones we ride around in. But the self is much more. It includes everything you think you are whether you are what you think you are or not. To a great extent, it is what you need to believe you are. It also includes a number of things you sometimes think of as being separate and apart from you. It includes your clothes, your political party, your beliefs in what sort of world this should be, your religion, and everything else you care about. Your caring, your feeling, and your concern determine whether or not something or somebody is part of your self.

The girl who rescues a child from drowning and the boy who volunteers to work for the Crisis Center answering service receive satisfaction from their service. For them, the self puts a value on such service. They are mature enough to sense a bond with others. They feel a need to serve.

We have all heard of acts of generosity and heroism described as "a giving of the self," as though some precious part of a person had been given up at a terrible loss to the self. But it is poor logic to portray such admirable behavior as "unselfish sacrifice." It tends to keep us from a clear view of what is going on.

A more sensible approach would be to recognize that generosity and heroism are very much in the interest of the self and to emphasize what this means: the self of a generous and courageous person has developed beyond the pettiness we commonly call "selfish." It has grown to a level of maturity, intelligence, and greatness where it senses the interrelation of the people of the world, where it feels concern, and where it experiences love.

Self-Picture—Don't Touch!

The self is sometimes thought of as a picture of what we think and feel we are. In this self-picture are all the things we value. If any part of it comes under attack, we react to defend it.

A threat against the self is feared as greatly as a threat against the physical body. When someone attempts to tear down the good picture we have of ourselves and of what we want to become, we may react as though our very lives were threatened.

We may try to avoid being degraded in front of our group as urgently as we would try to avoid a thug with a knife. An insulting word cuts deep. The psychic pain that comes from damage to the self-picture hurts as surely as the physical pain that comes from damage to the body. Being forced to view ourselves as something less than we want to be is a very painful experience.

Suppose a girl wants desperately to maintain a picture of herself as being pretty and attractive to the boys. If something belittling is said about her appearance, say a boy calls her, "Ugly, ugly," we can predict beforehand that this will have an emotional impact. It will likely make her angry, fearful, or a combination of both. Of course, she might conceal her feelings. Or she might show her feelings. We cannot predict for sure, but she might go so far as to slap someone or to turn and run.

In countless ways we try to avoid any damage to the self-picture, and we feel hurt and angry whenever such damage occurs.

Self-Consistency

Of course, it is not always someone else who threatens or damages our self-picture. Sometimes we do it ourselves. Sometimes we do things which are completely out of line with what we want to be.

And what are the consequences? As noted before, emotional reactions may be expected. Anger or fear or both may result—in this case, directed inwardly against ourselves or, sometimes, outwardly against other people when we refuse to let ourselves see who is truly to blame.

To be angry with ourselves and bent on self-punishment or to be afraid of ourselves is obviously an unhappy state of affairs—as is being unjustly angry and fearful toward others.

It should be clear that actions which are in conflict with what we want to be should be avoided. But there are reasons why this is not always possible. For one thing, the various ideas, attitudes, and loyalties within the self are not always consistent with one another. When we do right by one, we may do wrong by another. We have more than one role to play, and the expectations of different groups vary. At one time, with one group, we may feel we want to be one thing, and at another time with a different group, we may feel we want to be another. So here we have something else to guard against —letting ourselves get bogged down with unresolved conflicts within the self.

Briefly stated, if we are to gain happiness and peace of mind, we must act in a manner which goes along with being the type of people we know we want to be. But in order to do this, we have to know what we want to be. We have to know ourselves. We have to sit down and think things through from time to time and decide what is most important in our lives.

Conflict

Life is not a matter of simple clear-cut needs and motives. And our feelings about what we want to do are commonly in conflict with one another.

Sue wants a luscious, creamy dessert, but she also wants to keep a trim figure. Bill wants to maintain Shirley's affections, but at the same time he has been giving a lot of thought to a new girl who just transferred into school.

In our complex world of relatively free choice, we learn to want many things. Machines, more leisure time, and democratic institutions have enabled us to have a better, but by no means a simpler, life. We learn feelings of need for opposing things. As a result, we want, but at the same time we don't want. We want to approach, but at the same time we want to avoid.

Most of our conflicts present this *approach-avoidance* conflict. In this regard, two useful words to learn are *ambivalence* and *ambivalent*. When we are ambivalent toward something, we assign it valences of both plus and minus; that is, we feel both attraction and repulsion toward it.

Jean wants to live and enjoy life to its fullest, without restriction. She also wants to maintain a reputation and a self-picture above reproach. She is invited to a pajama party. She wants very much to go. The girls who invited her have never really accepted her before, and she wants them as friends. But she has heard that the party is going to be wild and that there will be some hard drugs around.

Manuel would like to be a doctor. He wants to be of service to people. He wants financial security. He wants status and position in his community. But he dislikes the idea of going to college so long and the requirements of getting top grades. He dreads going into debt for such prolonged schooling. And he would rather have more free time, instead of being on call day and night, as doctors are.

Both Jean and Manuel experience a strong feeling of ambivalence in their problem situations. They want, but knowing the consequences, they don't want. And before they are able to reach intelligent decisions on what to do, their conflicts may grow more intense and have increased complications.

Two experimental psychologists, Dollard and Miller, have described a characteristic of the approach-avoidance conflict that has application here. They point out that if the intensities of the desire to approach and the desire to avoid were plotted on a graph, both would be observed to increase as the subject neared the goal object, but the desire to avoid would have a steeper gradient. That is, the desire to avoid would rise more sharply than the desire to approach. In an approach-avoidance conflict situation, the two gradients would cross each other, and beyond that point of intersection the desire to avoid would rise above the desire to approach.

Applying this gradient to Jean's conflict, it can be predicted that her desire to avoid the party will increase much more sharply than she suspects as the time draws near. And if she attends, she may have resultant guilt feelings much greater than she could have imagined before the party.

As for Manuel, he may be well into his medical training before his desire to avoid causes him to change his plans and go into a field more to his liking—unless, of course, his increased interest may drive him on.

Another common example is the girl attracted to a boy who is not right for her. From a slight distance she is always attracted to him. But she has learned that when she goes out with him, nothing but trouble results. Each time she knows it is all wrong and wants desperately to get away. Then, after a time, she feels the attraction again. A glance at the plotted gradients suggests that the answer to such a dilemma is to get away and keep away. The less she has to do with him, the less she will sense the desire to approach. Fun for her is somewhere else.

Conflicts are a part of daily life. When they happen, they are not pleasant. They can hinder and limit our good times. Some hang on to plague us all our lives. But they are not all bad. We can learn and grow from them. And as we do, our capacity for deeper feelings increases. We gain the perspective necessary to decide what is most worthwhile in our lives.

The Conscious and the Unconscious

A very common limitation to the understanding of people and their behavior is the idea that we always act deliberately and know why we act. We assume that what we do is determined by *conscious, free will* guided by intelligent reason and logic.

This is a convenient idea, to be sure. It holds that each of us is responsible for what we do, and this seems only fair. Each of us deserves the credit or the blame, the reward or the punishment, for what we do.

This book does not deny the existence of free will. It encourages its increased use in place of blindly following the crowd. But it is not only our conscious, free will that determines what we do. There is a vast and active part of us operating on the unconscious level which influences behavior and of which we are more or less unaware.

I say *more or less*, because the various contents of the self are conscious or unconscious to varying degrees. The numerous bits of knowledge and impressions left by past experiences range from things of which we are constantly aware to things we may never remember.

Unconscious motivation has often been illustrated experimentally through post-hypnotic suggestion. For example, under hypnosis, a man was told that after he regained consciousness, a friend of his would be invisible to him until he heard the word "zero," at which time he was to slap his friend on the back. He was brought to a conscious state and shown a newspaper, which he was told to examine. He examined it—a perfectly normal newspaper. The newspaper was handed to his friend. For the next five minutes, not being able to see his friend, the subject tried to figure out what was making the paper float "in midair." Suddenly, the word "zero" was spoken, and to his surprise, he saw his friend and slapped him on the back. Asked why he had slapped his friend on the back, he said, "Because he played this trick on me. I don't know how he did it." Thus, the unconscious can influence not only what we do but also what we perceive.

It follows that since we are not always aware of our motivations, we are not always aware of our conflicts. And this does, indeed, complicate our world.

Have you ever gone on a date with someone who was mad about something but didn't know what?

Sometimes it is hard to have fun.

Chapter Five

SELF-DEFENSE

We do not want anyone cutting us down to less than we think we are. We do not want anyone hurting or belittling our family, friends, religion, city, country, school, car, clothes, political party, or any other person or thing we have made a part of the self. On the contrary, we want to build up the self. We want to be better than we were.

We attempt to defend and enhance the self in three general ways:

1. By attack or counterattack. This may take the form of destructive aggression or foolish bravado, or it may take the form of vigorous, intelligent action toward constructive goals.
2. By withdrawal, or running away from threatening or challenging situations.
3. By autistic restructuring; that is, by unconsciously changing the world and the self in our imagination and beliefs.

The specific defense mechanisms which we will consider in this chapter draw heavily on autistic restructuring. And autism must be understood in order to understand defense mechanisms.

Autism is the tendency for our needs to dominate the way we see and interpret things. We tend to see what we want to see and to believe what we want to believe. We tend to develop ideas and opinions that will defend and enhance the self and to reject ideas and opinions that will not defend and enhance the self.

This is not to say that we deliberately lie or twist the truth in order to favor the self. Autistic restructuring occurs automatically and unconsciously. When using defense mechanisms, we may be completely unaware of our errors in perception and judgment. And we may also be unaware that we are using defense mechanisms. This lack of awareness is an important element of defense mechanisms. Part of their purpose is to fool the self.

This is not necessarily bad if it is not done too long and too often. Each of us needs to be rescued from the hard facts of failure, disappointment, or tragedy, at least occasionally and temporarily. A low grade, a betrayal by a friend, or a death in the family takes time to face and accept.

Sometimes too many things happen at once, causing more threats to the self than we can cope with at one time. Our unconscious mechanisms step in to protect us and keep us from being overwhelmed. To this extent, defense mechanisms help us stay healthy.

Everyone uses defense mechanisms from time to time. There is nothing abnormal in their use. But defense mechanisms (also appropriately called *adjustment mechanisms*) do involve distortions of reality, and they must be understood if we are to understand our own behavior and the behavior of those around us. To be ignorant of their existence leads to confused thinking and to a need for additional defense mechanisms of our own.

As you will see, the categories are not clear-cut. The different defense mechanisms often overlap and are at work at the same time, one or another seeming to be most apparent when observed from different points of view.

Rationalization

Talk to a girl who sees herself as a future Hollywood actress but who has just been turned down for a part in the school play. Or talk with a boy who expects to go into professional sports but who fumbled the ball in the critical minutes of the biggest game of the year. You are likely to hear an emotional, exaggerated view of what "really" happened. The explanation might be so far out that it is hard to believe. It might best be called a *rationalization* rather than an explanation.

Rationalizing is the very common defense of bringing in a system of reasoning and apparent logic to defend the self or, sometimes, to support other defense mechanisms being used.

Once again, it must be remembered that this is an unconscious mechanism, as are all defense mechanisms. Rationalizing is not a matter of making up alibis. At least, it is not that to the person doing it. He is unconscious of the fact that his explanations are slanted and false.

Repression

Another way we commonly fool ourselves is through a mechanism of active forgetting called *repression*. Occasionally, there are things too frightening, threatening, or uncomfortable to think about, and our unconscious mechanisms push these things "out of mind."

Carol was driving when the accident occurred, killing her little sister and a neighbor girl. Except for minor bruises, Carol was unharmed. But for weeks afterward, she was unable to recall anything about the accident. She remembered driving and the fun they were having. She remembered what happened up to a few minutes before the accident. But she could remember nothing of the accident or its horrible aftermath. Through repression, the conscious self was defended from the terrible knowledge that she was responsible for the deaths of the little girls.

There are many less extreme cases of repression. We may find it difficult to remember an unpleasant class assignment or a feared dental appointment. We may not be able to find some article of clothing when we are dressing for a dreaded date. Through such repressions we frequently attempt to evade the minor threats of daily living. We conveniently "forget."

Of course, it can be shown that repressed material is not miraculously eliminated. It is only pushed down to a relatively unconscious level, where it may continue to influence behavior in subtle ways. This is a keystone in psychoanalysis and understanding behavior in depth.

Note that, as a general rule, it is not wise to press anyone to recall things he has apparently forgotten, especially things associated with feelings of inadequacy or guilt. When this must be done, it should be in the hands of a psychiatrist or skilled analyst. When memories are repressed, they are repressed for a purpose.

Reaction Formation

Have you ever known a boy and a girl who told everyone how much they hated each other—and then started going together? To begin with, they may have taken every opportunity to ridicule, to list the other's faults, to hurt, and to show they did not care. Then, something changed, and they cared very much. How do you suppose their feelings could have changed so radically, so suddenly?

One possible answer is that there was no change in their true feelings, deep down. They may have been strongly attracted to each other all along but somehow did not know it. For some reason, it was threatening and unacceptable to feel that they cared for each other. They may have been afraid of not being loved in return. This is a common and often realistic fear. Or they may have been going steady with other people and felt conflicting obligations at the time. There may have been a number of reasons why feeling love for the other was unacceptable to the self. They could not let themselves experience this temporarily forbidden love. And to keep from feeling it, they felt the opposite. We see a similar reaction among grammar school boys who torment the girls they like the most.

This defense of the self is known as a *reaction formation*. It is one of the most emotion-loaded mechanisms of all. In reaction formation, we fool ourselves into believing we have feelings toward somebody or something which are completely the opposite of what we unconsciously feel. And nothing could be more objectionable than to realize that we unconsciously feel the opposite of what we believe we feel. As a consequence, anyone who tampers with this defense will be met with every additional defense that can be mustered, including aggression.

Regression

It is no cinch to grow up. Many so-called adults have never made the grade. Growing up means more than owning a car, having a job, or talking big about being able to do your own thing. It means facing life. It means taking on responsibility—not just for ourselves, but to some extent for those we love and for the world around us. No wonder we occasionally defend ourselves through *regression*.

Regression means going back to an earlier (usually happier) period of our lives or to an earlier stage of development. That is, in regression we act and think as we did in some period when we were younger. When the self is severely threatened, our progress toward maturity may seem inadequate and of very little value. We may slip back into our near or distant past, reviving responses and behavior we had previously discarded.

Too vividly, I remember a fellow paratrooper in the France of World War II. One moment, he was a whole and vigorous man, and the next, after the explosion of an enemy shell, he was a crumpled form on the ground, crying, "Mama! Mama!"

To take more modern examples:

Stu gave up smoking when he started going with Marge. The night Marge jilted him, he slipped back to smoking again. Sydney lost the class election, and minutes later at her locker, she threw her books in so hard they bounced out onto the floor. She threw them back again, kicked the door, and started to cry.

Indeed, there remains much of the child still within us. We grow and work toward the kind of person we want to be. But when things go wrong, it is often a struggle to keep from giving way to the old, immature impulses of childhood.

Dissociation

George and his girl friend are legally old enough to be out on their own. They live in San Francisco and declare they do not need anything or anybody. The checks that come from the girl's mother for them to live on, the rides they thumb when traveling, the police protection they have called on in order to survive, and the health clinic—these are much as rain and trees to them all the while they assert their complete independence from and contempt for the establishment.

Lisa preaches ecology and plans to be a public health nurse. But at home, she is careless when emptying the garbage, even though she knows there is a problem with rats in the neighborhood. She ignores litter in the halls and grumbles when asked by her grandmother to help clean the house.

Our attitudes, values, actions, and the realities of life are not always neatly consistent with one another. Far from it! Occasionally, there are distinct conflicts which may be kept from the self through a repressive mechanism known as *dissociation*.

Fred complains that the teacher is unfair in her methods of grading, unfair in calling on some students more often than others, unfair in not explaining some things a second time, and on and on. But he turns a blind eye to his discourtesies that disrupt the class, to his copying his girl friend's homework, and to his open cheating on exams.

Jeanne speaks out righteously in her civics class, condemning prejudice against blacks. But she snubs the Indian girl who sits across the aisle. In her own clique, she expresses the same generalized prejudices against American Indians that she feels other people express against blacks. But she does not associate these conflicting attitudes with each other.

Instead of *associating* the related situations or ideas in our thinking, which could result in more intelligent living, sometimes we do the opposite. In order to protect the self, we *dissociate* them, blinding ourselves to the inconsistencies and contradictions in our behavior, and thereby avoiding the shame and guilt feelings that can come from knowing the truth. We keep the logic as seen from one point of view from coming to grips with the logic as seen from another point of view. We develop what has been called a system of "logic-tight compartments."

By keeping contradictory attitudes and actions separated in their logic-tight compartments, we protect the self from the worrisome conflicts in the short run—and we keep the self from growth and sound health in the long run.

Projection

Back in the paratroops, I remember there were always men who did a lot of talking about how some other guys were going to "freeze in the door" and be afraid to jump. It was no secret to anyone except the big talkers that they themselves were frightened and worried about whether or not they would be able to muster enough courage to make the next jump.

Whenever we have traits which are inconsistent with the self-picture, we tend to see these objectionable traits in others much more than is warranted. This makes it possible for us to feel that we are much better by comparison. Busy criticizing other people, we avoid seeing ourselves as we are. The defense mechanism here comes under the heading of *projection*—projecting unworthy feelings, traits, or impulses onto another person.

A common example during our teen years occurs when we blame our parents for things which are much more our fault than theirs. Too often we let ourselves act like little children, and we certainly do not want to admit this even to ourselves. When our parents correct us and point out the childishness of our behavior, we feel this is unwarranted and unfair. We avoid seeing our own blame by projecting the blame for the trouble between us onto our parents. We say they are always nagging us and griping without cause. We complain that "they treat us like kids," and we refuse to see that our behavior forces them to do just that. (I hasten to recognize that not all conflict between teens and parents is the fault of teens. But neither is it always the fault of the parents. Projection flows both ways. Everyone projects from time to time.)

Almost magically, in some cases, our actions have a way of making the traits we project and imagine in other people become realities. What we project in our imagination often grows there, even when it was not there before we projected it.

Take the individual who, for some reason or other, does not like people. He projects this feeling and imagines that other people do not like him. Then, naturally, he scowls, shows suspicion, and in other ways acts as though people do not like him. And in no time, sure enough, he is right—people do not like him.

Happily, this process also can work the other way. Projection is not always a negative mechanism. For the relatively happy, mature self, projection makes the world a better place in which to live. For the person who believes it is a grand and friendly world and acts accordingly, the chances are increasingly in favor of its being exactly that—a grand and friendly world.

Chapter Six

MORE SELF-DEFENSE

Displaced Aggression and Scapegoating

In prehistoric times when the cave dwellers were confronted with threats to their survival, they did one of two things. Either they fought and won, or they ran and got away. Since these aggressive and withdrawal reactions—sometimes called *fight* and *flight*—have been around for a long time, it is not surprising to find them as common reactions to modern-day threats to the self. But most of us have learned that the basic reactions of prehistoric cave dwellers do not always pay off in civilization. Bare aggression usually leads only to additional frustration.

Most of us have learned to take strong criticism from a teacher, coach, or sergeant rather than strike back with angry insults. We jump out of the way of an oncoming truck rather than swing at it with our fists. We try to avoid a gang of toughs armed with knives and chains rather than invite pointless combat. However, we still have aggressive feelings at such times. Frustration pushes us toward aggression. We *feel* like fighting *something*. And if it is impractical or impossible for us to strike at the true source of our frustration, we may strike at something else. That is, we may *displace* aggression from the actual source of frustration to other people or objects.

Chuck is pushed around by a bigger boy on the ball field. Soon after, he hits a smaller boy who accidentally bumps into him in the hallway. Lee Ann arrives home after being snubbed by other girls at school, and for no apparent reason she calls her younger sister "stupid" and says her new dress makes her look "sloppy fat."

When asked for explanations of their behavior, both Chuck and Lee Ann may use rationalizations to justify themselves. Chuck might say, and believe, that the boy bumped into him on purpose and deserved to be hit. Lee Ann might say, and believe, that her younger sister needed to be told the truth about her clothes so she would have better sense about what she wore.

Chuck and Lee Ann are using *scapegoats.* Unconsciously, they are putting blame for the way they feel on those against whom they can take revenge with less fear. There is nothing new in this. The term "scapegoat" comes from the practice of ancient tribes placing their sins on a goat, then killing the goat. More recent examples of displaced aggression supported by rationalization include the burning of "witches" in Salem and the persecution of the Jews in Nazi Germany.

When they feel threatened, the ignorant and immature seek out scapegoats. They give vent to their most aggressive impulses and pretend they are doing something about their problems. They believe, at least for a time, that they are completely justified in what they do. But surely, the use of scapegoats is one of the most unjust things people have been known to do. The torture of a defenseless animal, the mistreatment of a racial or religious group, the ridiculing of a handicapped boy or girl, and the burning of a "witch" are shameful among people who would be called civilized.

The tendency to displace aggression or scapegoat is in us all. Understanding it for what it is helps keep it from getting out of hand.

Fantasy

The flight reaction is as well known to us as the fight reaction. We have all known the feeling of wanting to turn and run away from challenging or threatening situations. But we also know that there are times when literally running away is not the thing to do. The student in a class he does not enjoy may feel like getting up and walking out. But he probably will not, no matter how bored and defeated he may feel. He knows the consequences. The girl bitterly unhappy with her home life may feel like running away. But chances are she will not. Intelligence will tell her that running away can lead to tragedy or, at best, a worsening of her circumstances.

Wise or not, we all feel the need to escape at times. And we do escape in ways less obvious to those around us, in ways that do not have such severe consequences. To escape the threats and unpleasantness of the world as it is, we slip off into a world of daydreams. We gain satisfaction through our imagination, through *fantasy*.

The uninterested or failing student may let his thoughts drift to fantasies of pleasure and success. He may daydream of the fun he hopes to have on the weekend with the guys. He may daydream of winning the girl across the aisle by rescuing her from fierce pirates. He may daydream of being a professional man with status in his community—while in reality he is ignoring the basic education he requires to be self-supporting. There is no limit to the extent or the number of daydreams.

The unhappy girl may imagine herself doing all the things she wants to do and having everything she wants. She may daydream of loving and being loved, exquisitely, surrounded by perfection—even while she is doing things that make it less and less possible for her to find lasting love and happiness.

Compensation

No one gets everything he wants. We all face disappointments. Ruth's steady boyfriend left her for another girl. Sam did not pass the entrance exam for the college of his choice. Judy did not make cheerleader. Steve was turned down by the girl he wanted to take to the prom.

A relatively healthy answer to such frustrations is to seek out a substitute to *compensate* for the first choice which is not available.

Ruth found another boy. Sam selected a less-crowded college. Judy spent more time on her studies and raised her grades. Steve took another girl to the prom.

With a little luck, the second choice may be completely satisfying and may come to be genuinely preferred over the first choice. Then there is no need for defensive behavior. But unfortunately, sometimes the original first choice is not replaced. It continues, unconsciously, as the first choice, covered up by rationalizations. When this happens, the constant basic lack of satisfaction increases the need for compensation. It may lead to *overcompensation* and to ridiculous extremes in attempting to prove the second choice better than the first.

All too common are the kids who try to compensate for disadvantages or lack of status and success by acting tough, calling people "chicken," and getting themselves and others in trouble. It is a safe bet that this behavior is not their first choice. Deep down, perhaps so deep they keep it secret even from their own awareness, they want to live a more sensible life. The toughness is a second choice. This makes it doubly important for them to show the world how dumb it is to go to school and follow rules. They work overtime trying to fool themselves. They overcompensate.

Sometimes overcompensation goes so far as to blend with reaction formation. Take, for example, a girl who wants desperately to be beautiful, but clearly is not. She might compensate by trying to be the ugliest, by wearing baggy clothes and shaping her hair in shaggy, off-beat ways. She might be outspoken in showing contempt for pretty girls and for "the nutty boys who fall for all the superficial nonsense." Her emotional displays in trying to prove her arguments against good looks and femininity betray her overcompensation and reaction formation.

Of course, compensation is not always negative or destructive. Quite the contrary. One of the greatest secrets of success in life is realizing that lack of good fortune in one area can contribute to good fortune in another. The frustrated person can turn to constructive use the energy released by his aggressive impulses.

Obviously, not all disadvantaged kids try to compensate by acting tough or getting into trouble. Far from it. Some compensate for their unfortunate situations by trying to do better in school, by going out for sports, or by becoming active in a club. Instead of slipping toward a life of waste and crime, they work toward being an athlete, a scientist, a social worker, or some other career with positive purpose. Similarly, the energy of a repressed sex urge can be turned to creative work. A boy or girl attempting to keep sexual desires in check can find personal satisfaction and release of tension through activity in sports, music, writing, or art.

Compensation of this sort, whether for aggressive or sexual urges, is known as *sublimation*—the channeling of the energy of an anti-social urge into socially acceptable activities.

Identification

In an apparent life-or-death struggle to defend the self, some mechanisms are offensive to other people and actually destructive to the self. In contrast, other mechanisms, such as sublimation, are more likely to be constructive and to contribute to the well-being of other people and the healthy development of the self.

Among the mechanisms which are more often constructive than destructive is *identification*. When we use this mechanism, we identify with other persons, groups, or objects; that is, we make them a part of the self. And as a result, we experience a personal satisfaction in their accomplishments.

Applying a touch of fantasy, we use identification each time we read a story or watch one on television or at the movies. We enjoy the story to the extent that we can identify with the characters and their goals. We receive satisfaction in the triumph of the characters we have made a part of the self. And when real life seems filled with threats and defeats, we feel better because of our refreshing sessions of identification with these daring characters who always win out in the end. Of course, we tend to identify more lastingly with real people than with fictional characters. The more real they are to us and the more they do what we would like to do, the more likely we are to identify with them.

Lois wanted to be petite and pretty and sought-after by the boys. She was not. She identified with a girl friend who was and thrilled at hearing of her romantic adventures. Joe was slight of build and felt bullied and pushed around. He wanted power and strength and revenge on the world. In a confused way, he identified with Hitler, reading all the books he could find about the Nazis and displaying a swastika on his bedroom wall.

Whether or not identification is destined to help or hurt the self depends greatly on the person, group, or object with whom we identify. We may identify with a loving father and mother, a scientist, a teacher, a national hero, a coach, a 4-H leader, an Explorer Scout adviser, a school team, a religion. Or we may identify with a criminal, a chronic failure, a fast-talking con man, a would-be dictator, an unemployed dropout, a gang bent on theft and vandalism, a ruthless political doctrine. The consequences will be quite different in terms of our makeup as a person.

Introjection

Closely related to identification is the mechanism called *introjection.*

George has a problem. He is hanging out with a gang of boys whose code is in harsh conflict with the teachings of his religion. One path for him is to identify completely with the gang and to accept its code and the rule of its leaders without question. Another is to identify completely with his religion and to accept its teachings without question. Either of these possible attempts to escape conflict is an example of introjection *if entered into blindly.*

Introjection is accepting as our own the attitudes, values, and goals of other people without logically arriving at the conclusion that these attitudes, values, and goals are sound. This defense mechanism is somewhat the opposite of projection. You will recall that in projection we shape the world to suit the self. In introjection we shape the self to suit the world.

To get along, all of us have learned to introject to some extent, perhaps more than we realize. As evidence of this, we may passionately defend political parties or religions which we claim as ours but know next to nothing about. The question is, do we believe and act as we do because of conclusions based on logical understanding or inspired faith, or because of mere introjection supported by makeshift rationalizations? There is danger ahead for the self defended greatly by introjections. These defenses cannot stand concentrated attack. Sometimes they topple from their own weight.

A Word of Warning

Recognizing defense mechanisms in another person can help us to understand him and to act wisely in regard to him. But it should be clear by now that calling his defense mechanisms to his attention seldom causes anything but trouble. Attempting to reveal these mechanisms for what they are is an attack on the person's self-picture and will result in his emotional scramble to defend his defenses.

Use your new-found concepts and symbols to think and act intelligently. But know your limitations. Do not try to play analyst or psychiatrist any more than you would try to play surgeon.

Although defense mechanisms may seem objectionable to an outside observer, they have important purposes on an unconscious level for the person using them. When we challenge defense mechanisms and try to force them into the open for conscious examination, new defenses are thrown up to protect or replace the old ones—and the new defenses may turn out to be even more objectionable. Attacking defense mechanisms must be reserved for times when they are seriously infringing on the rights of others.

Chapter Seven

ACTION

"I should have called her or gone over there or something," the tall boy says angrily, more to himself than to me. "I wanted to. Instead I just sat there doing nothing."

Unrelated, two minutes later a teacher stops me in the hall and says, "I know Anne has problems. But regardless, I can't take the way she's acting in my classes. See that she settles down, will you? I don't want to have to take her to the principal."

Every school day for the past twenty years, I have talked with people whose problems came under the heading of *action*. Some came to talk on their own. Some were invited. But the basic problem expressed was at least partly a matter of getting into action or of putting on the brakes and stopping the action—a matter of turning on or turning off.

It is difficult to find the switch, the magic go-stop-go button. Getting into motion or trying to hold back and keep from doing something is very much a matter of internal control. With all sorts of limitations, counselors provide opportunities and information to enable people to make sound decisions about the actions they wish to take. But counselees, not counselors, have control of their own individual activation.

Another mistaken idea is that counselors always try to cut down the action, that they try to adjust people into some sort of contented-cow status where they are completely at ease and cause no trouble or distraction to those around them.

Of course, there are times when the best advice is, "Cool it. And breed peace." But it is a phony idea that people are happy and well-adjusted only when they have attained a serene, vegetable-like existence. In the long run, sitting happily satisfied and enjoying contentment is a brief, temporary experience. Life is not all a matter of striving for satisfaction and trying to become adjusted. An undeniable portion of life is the slipping toward dissatisfaction and becoming unadjusted. At times, we intentionally throw ourselves off-balance or out of adjustment—and not always with great sorrow or lack of fun.

Remember the story of the what-me-worry type who sat on a tack because it felt so good to get up? There is something of this kid in all of us. In a rather complex way, this tendency to unadjust as well as to adjust is very much a part of each of us.

We read stories and go to movies and identify with the protagonists. With them we suffer all sorts of conflict and stress, so we can enjoy the happy endings. We go camping and rough it, so we can enjoy the feeling of accomplishment and self-worth that comes with surviving under adverse circumstances. We work hard in high school so we can earn and enjoy a fulfilling life tomorrow. We do all these things and many more for the rewards of satisfaction. But we do them for another reason as well. We do them because of the tendency or drive within us toward *action*.

All of us have known this common experience: we reach one goal, we get something we genuinely wanted or needed, but instead of remaining satisfied and enjoying our attainment to the fullest, we soon feel restless. We start to long for new activities and new satisfactions. Our choice of activity at such times is extremely important. We are wide open to challenging opportunities of both the happy and unhappy varieties.

Some people find a new line of books in the library. Some seek new friends. Some climb mountains. Some compete in athletics. Some work in hospitals and day-care centers. Some organize clean-up projects on the block. Some work diligently toward long-term goals with reasonable, constructive purposes.

But some do quite the opposite. Some are wiped out when it comes to doing much of anything constructive. Instead of letting this drive toward action work for them and for the betterment of their world, they do seemingly pointless, ridiculous things. They even hurt people and destroy the hard-won accomplishments of others in their wild attempts to be doing something.

The direction of the action is all important. On the one extreme there are people at work getting it together—with love, building the best way they can. On the other, there are the bitter, raving destroyers tearing things down—with hate, trying to convince themselves that in a world of ashes and rotting corpses things will automatically be better.

So where do we go? What is going to make for success and fun for you and yours? Where do you put the action?

Let's explore further.

Vandalism

The destructive exploits of the Vandals, those vengeful Aryan Christians who terrorized the Mediterranean and pillaged Rome in the fifth century, may have been exaggerated somewhat. But it is said that behind them lay a smoldering waste of shattered art objects, wrecked churches, slashed paintings, and gutted buildings that forever earned them the reputation for wanton destruction of beauty.

Needless to say, the aggressions of war and conquest have always brought destruction. It is a bit more difficult to comprehend that we have vandals here and now. From time to time, there are those even in your own school who earn the name of vandal. Like barbarians, they lash out and destroy property. More accurately, like *small children*, they give free vent to their hostile impulses. No place is safe from them, it seems, and no place sanctified.

Not long ago, I had the fun of taking my sister on her first visit to Yellowstone National Park. She is blind. And a planned highlight was a visit to the new Three Senses nature trail at Firehole Lake that had been completed just a week earlier. This new trail had been constructed so that a blind person can go the length of it alone, following the railing and stopping at the many points of interest to read the Braille messages on the metal plaques.

Steam from the hot lake drifted across the path that bright afternoon. Vi led the way, telling us of the things she sensed and reading aloud the Braille signs along the way. The natural feeling was, of course, that there should be many more such trails in the world.

Halfway through the trail, however, there were other feelings. Vandals had defaced and poked holes in a number of the plaques meant to provide the Braille messages. Some of the Braille dots had been rubbed out, making the messages difficult or impossible to read.

Tragically, vandals continually limit our chances for fun and actually threaten survival. Too often, even when they are caught, they are not required to make amends. They shout "unfair" when someone tries to make them pay damages. But their destruction of the work of others is one of the most unfair forces in the country today. Why?

Some blame parental neglect. But in addressing teenagers, blaming the parents is senseless. For one thing, it is not just the kids doing it. And if it were, it would be their responsibility, not their parents, and they—you—will have the crummy world vandalism creates: schools that look like fortresses under siege, ugly restrooms, obscenities on every wall, higher prices and taxes to keep up repairs, lack of public phones in emergencies, but worst of all, more and more people who simply do not give a damn.

"Why try to have anything nice?" you must have heard said by now. "You work hard for something, and then some numbhead comes along and messes it up."

Terrible to admit, perhaps, but sometimes we are the enemy. There are tendencies toward such immature action in all of us. Anger and resentment are common feelings. Everyone has sensed the desire to get even and take revenge for the everyday injustice and unfairness in the world.

This being the case, it seems logical that, individually, we need to keep ourselves under enough control in our drive toward action and fun that we do not give way to compounding our problems by acting destructively; and that collectively we develop ways of protecting ourselves and our property from those people who run wild from time to time and who blindly take revenge for their troubles on anybody or anything in sight.

Action with Purpose

Everything a person does has a purpose. Take schoolwork, for example. Think of what you are working for in school. You better have a number of answers. If you do not, school is not going to be much fun, and it is going to be much more difficult for you than it has to be.

If you cannot come up with reasons for working in school, you may have begun to let yourself be bogged down with reasons for *not* working in school. You may even now be coming up with the old, trite bit about being "lazy," the idea that somehow lying down on the job in school gets you out of work. And nothing could be further from the truth. Many students spend twice as much energy trying to get out of work as they would if they promptly tackled the work to be done. Some repeat whole courses because they wasted their energies the first time around. Some drop out of school to evade work but then find that they have *dropped in* to something much less pleasant —hard work (if they can find it) and little pay.

So one obvious reason for working in school is a smart form of "laziness." Working in school can mean less work and more fun in the long run. The higher your grades, the better your chances for recognition and success in later life.

Another reason for working in school is your natural interest in the opposite sex. Far out? Not really. Any reasonable hope of both winning the boy or girl of your choice and having the sort of life you will want together rests on *preparation*. Some measure of success in your schoolwork is an indispensable part of this needed preparation.

But perhaps the best reasons you can have are found in the answers to these questions: "What do you want to be?" and "What kind of a world do you want this to be?" Becoming what you want to be and making this the sort of world you want it to be are worth working for in school. And if you do not have the answers to such questions, it is worth your effort to find them. Being active in school makes both the present and the future more fun.

Reversing Wrong-Way Action

Some habits get in the way of having fun. But before setting out to change habits, it is always wise to think about where we are headed. Certainly, some of our habits may not be the best. But there is a chance that some of our habits could be worse. What better habits do we plan to put in the place of the old ones? In this question lies the key to successfully breaking bad habits.

The emphasis should be on changing to something good, not just on escaping from something bad. We cannot eliminate a bad habit and just leave a vacuum. Something must and will come in to take its place—something better, something worse, or the same old habit, just as strong as ever.

Suppose you have the habit of biting your nails. When do you bite your nails? All the time? Or just when you are a little tense, worried, excited? Well, then what do you suppose you could do with your hands at these times instead of bite your nails? Twist a handkerchief? Kind of expensive, but perhaps better than eating your fingers. Perhaps you could take up knitting. How about fingering a string of paper clips, some rubber bands, or a little rubber animal toy? Seems a little silly, but it is better than nail biting. So if nail biting is a problem, the next time you go to a tense movie, sit down to watch TV, or start to study for that test you are worried about, try putting the wear and tear on a piece of cloth or a string of paper clips instead of your fingers.

Suppose you and your friends have the habit of doing some things around the neighborhood that are bound to get you into trouble. What can you find to do that would steer you away from trouble and actually be more fun? How about getting started in a youth group, such as the Explorers or the Y?

Or suppose you fight with your brother. How about running around the block instead? Or how about both of you beginning a physical fitness course? This way you would work off steam with constructive results. In any event, you cannot solve action problems with inactivity.

Extracurricular Activities

There is much to be said for the well-rounded life, one that includes a sampling of a wide variety of activities, both in student years and in later life.

Surely, most of us would agree that school should be more than

academic work and study. And in most schools opportunities abound
—football, yearbook staff, newspaper photographers, track, pep band,
stagecraft, service clubs, cheerleaders, science club, debate, drama,
wrestling, gymnastics, chess club, student council, glee club, literary
club, AVA assistants, and basketball, to name a few. It can pay to
take a look at what is available and participate in one or more activities. But there are limitations.

On the one extreme, the loner would probably find more happiness and satisfaction if he could bring himself to enter into some
activities. And at the other extreme, the joiner would probably be
better off to restrict the number of memberships and contribute
more to fewer activities.

Some students find more than enough to do outside of school in
part-time jobs, Explorer Specialty Oriented Posts, 4-H, political and
religious concerns, ecological projects, and family activities. Some
have very little activity outside of school. And still others find that
it works out for them to participate in extracurricular activities at
school in addition to continuing in outside activities.

The old concept of individual differences is important here. To
each his own is the rule. An activity which is significant to one may
not be worth the bother to someone else. However, one good reason
for joining an activity is to discover and explore a new area of possible interest. Most activities are of potential interest to most people
if entered into with an open mind. Unfortunately, a lot of phony
rationalizations are aired as people defend their inabilities to enter
into activities, and this creates considerable faulty prejudging.

Joining an activity, regardless of the reason for joining, also involves the acceptance of the obligations of membership. How many
people do you know who ran for student body office and did not
do much of anything after they were elected? Whether it is joining
a special interest club, being a member of the student council, or
going out for track, it is more than just an honor, a privilege, or
maybe another picture in the yearbook. It is a responsibility. It requires loyalty and work.

Extracurricular activities can contribute greatly to your fun in life,
but only if they are truly activities for you, things that fulfill the
first element of the fun formula—the need for *action*.

Chapter Eight

DISCOVERY AND LEARNING

Perhaps the most significant discovery of all is learning. Learning about learning is basic to a full and fun-filled life.

The many complexities of psychological learning theory are beyond the space limitations of this book, but one pervasive tendency requires emphasis: *we learn and remember things that are personally meaningful to us.*

Our brain and nervous system make up a fabulous sorting system, processing millions of decisions on what is worth our attention and what is not. Each day we pass by an endless series of minor stimulations that we barely notice and do not remember. Think of all the books in the libraries, all of interest to someone or another, that you scanned until something really caught your eye. Remember all the titles? Or what about the desk in your Third Period class? What do you know about it? How was it made, do you suppose? Is the seat curved? How did they do that? Do you wonder if the craftsmen were women or men? Do you wonder if they were proud of their work?

Of course, there is no need to know or to learn all that. The built-in selectivity of our personal thinking machines serves a useful purpose in keeping us from being bogged down with pointless trivia. It works well, for the most part. Much depends on how it is programmed. Some things we cannot afford to ignore as much as others.

If, for example, I called you into my office and told you how to fill out a form to apply for something you did not care much about, you might learn how to complete the form correctly or you might not. But if I called you in and told you that Big Eldredge thinks you said some crude things about him and he was going to be laying for you after school, you would remember that! We tend to learn very quickly those things that have to do with our survival. *We learn and remember things that are personally meaningful to us.*

But we hold back from learning some things. Some things we have to learn to feel a personal meaningfulness about. And unfortunately, nearly all of us have some short circuits in our computer when it comes to learning. To one extent or another, we are all victims of negative learning. We have learned at least a few things that simply are not true.

Those who say, "There's nothing to do in this town," are often among the people who are not interested in learning and discovery. And as a consequence they are not having much fun. They are turned off to many of the fun things around them. They may not have even discovered school as a part of the total fun scene. They may view it as some sort of enemy. They may have slipped to scape-goating teachers and fellow students for their own unwillingness to enter in. And then, a self-fulfilling prophecy comes into play. When they act like school cannot be fun for them, they prove themselves correct.

But it does not have to be that way. What does it take to have fun and success at school? What stands in the way?

Obstacles to Academic Learning

One common reason we do not learn as easily as we might lies in an ambivalent attitude toward schoolwork. We want, but at the same time we don't want. We want to be doing more than one thing, but we can only be doing one thing at a time. We want to do the schoolwork and to gain the rewards that can result from doing it well. But it is *work*. And often there are other, more comfortable things we would prefer doing.

Another obstacle to the process of learning is that we have learned not to learn. Some of us have learned to turn off at times when we should turn on. This is true of all of us to some extent. We have learned to be "lazy." That is, we have learned to try to avoid work. In school and out, we have learned habits that interfere with efficient, rapid learning.

For many of us, the most difficult part of studying is getting with it. We have trouble making ourselves get started. Instead of accepting the assignment the instructor gives us, we resist it. We put off doing it, as though we hope some magic will occur and little elves will step in and do it for us.

A third obstacle to learning is the autistic restructuring we use in defending the self. We are inclined to believe what we need to believe. We are inclined to see what we need to see. We want to protect the self and the self-picture, and we act and learn accordingly.

Again, there is self-fulfilling prophecy at work. If we believe that we are slow in a subject, we play it that way, whether the mental machinery makes this necessary or not. A girl who says, "I just know I won't do well in geometry; math is real hard for me," will be inclined to prove herself correct. Her belief that she is slow in math will tend to make her slow. The boy who says, "I can't get that grammar; I can't see any sense to it," is also inclined to prove himself correct. His belief that he can't get grammar will tend to keep him from getting it.

Also linked to self-defense are the distortions that occur as we try to interpret subject matter and fit it into a meaningful position in our memory patterns to guide our future behavior.

The boy who has been taught by his father that a particular race or political party is superior to all others will tend to interpret everything from biology to history in such a way as to support his beliefs. Ideas in conflict with his beliefs will tend to be rejected or distorted. A girl who has been taught that men, sex, and romantic love are basically evil will tend to interpret things in such a way as to support her beliefs. Passages in literature intended to be tender and intimate may seem to her coarse and wicked. Revealing discussions of wholesome married life may seem shocking and dirty.

Lastly, this list of obstacles to learning would not be complete if we did not mention the hierarchy of needs (discussed in Chapter

Three). Underachievement and failure in school cannot be understood without some knowledge of the needs and feelings of the individuals involved.

A number of teens are still in a tangle of confused learning patterns left over from childhood, when they found they could get more attention by failing in schoolwork. In the lower grades and, perhaps, in competition with a number of brothers and sisters, they felt a strong need for more attention and expressions of love than they received from their parents. They may have worked to win praise but found to their disappointment that the hard-earned B's and C's brought brief half-praise, at best, or the reproving "Why can't you get A's like your sister or like Louis down the street?" There was no success, no point in trying. Then, by accident or on purpose, they fell down in their work.

An 8-year-old, telling his problems to a psychotherapist, put it this way: "I tried and tried to please them, and all they ever did was tell me I could do better. But then I started getting F's and D's. And they started having conferences with my teacher and the principal. And I got called in to take tests, special ones. Mom clears off the table after supper and sends all the other kids out of the kitchen. And she helps me. They're really worried about me, now. Afraid I might not make it in school."

Then failure becomes success and success becomes failure. If it takes failure in school to get attention, some children will oblige. Remember the hierarchy of needs. There are needs that come before our need to succeed in school, especially in elementary school.

In high school, a great many teens still are more concerned with gaining the attention of their parents or their teachers than with learning and achieving. Some are falling short to "get even" with their parents or their teachers. "If I don't like a teacher, I won't work for her," some students explain. And such students are sadly dependent on their teachers for success in school. If they like a teacher, they work. If they don't, they won't. They have not developed a sense of need to prepare for the future. They have missed the fact that the accomplishment of learning can be fun, with or without the affection of a teacher.

Problems, Problems, Problems

"Fun? Don't expect me to have fun tonight. (Moan, groan.) I've got problems!"

A person can become overwhelmed. But for the most part, fun does not have to stop because a person has problems. Working out solutions to problems is a learning experience and can often be fun in itself. Through problem-solving we learn how to make things better, to earn things we want to have, and to appreciate the many things around us that we have already.

But the ideas we hold about problems can make it difficult for us to deal with them intelligently. If, for example, we relate an unwarranted sense of guilt and shame to having problems, we may repress realities and erect distorting defenses that in turn can cause greater difficulties than suffered in the first place.

It is natural to feel exaggerated impact for our own concerns, and just as natural to feel that no one else has problems quite like our own. And it is true that our problems are unique, up to a point. However, there are general problems that we have in common with our friends, and we can gain much from sharing ideas and possible solutions with other members of our group. Quite often we gain insight and peace of mind merely from learning that we are not alone in how we feel. Open discussions can help. And there is fun in the process. Both the helping and the being helped are learning experiences to be enjoyed.

Here, as with all good things, of course, there must be limitations. Certainly your most personal concerns are not for large group discussions. Some problems are best discussed only in private talks with a special trusted few—trusted both to be able to genuinely help and to be able to keep confidences.

The need for help is most urgent when problems are extremely confidential and, at the same time, when the secrets are hard for other people to keep. Unhappily, many friendships have been shattered by betrayals. Do not blunder out your most sacred feelings or the most shameful experiences of your life in group games or to someone you know to be a gossip. If you have a close friend, a brother, or a sister whom you respect and trust, or a parent with whom you can talk, you are fortunate. If not, think about talking to your doctor, religious leader, or school counselor.

What About School Counselors?

Although confidentiality laws vary from state to state, most schools have counselors who provide confidential settings where students may discuss their individual concerns and seek learning that may not be appropriate for the class room. Ann Landers, incidentally, has told me that she has never had anything but praise for school counselors after referring young people to them for help.

School counselors, sometimes called *guidance counselors*, first of all, are people. They are people who care about people. Most of them are former teachers who have taken additional graduate training and have been selected because of their capacities and interests in providing helping relationships for students. Unfortunately, some of us do not come off as favorably as we would like. In the vast majority of schools, counselors have job loads that range from overwhelming to impossible.

The 1971 White House Conference on Youth formally recommended: "Counselors should (a) devote a major share of their time and effort to facilitating the student's personal, cultural, and environmental exploration, career and life style planning and decision-making and building multiple choices within the curriculum, (b) be available in sufficient numbers to work with all students throughout elementary and secondary schools (one counselor to 50 students), (c) be made more readily available to *all* students. The roles of these counselors should be defined at the local level with participation from the students to be served, the employers, and the counselors. The primary concern of counselors should be the worth and well-being of the students. Therefore, counselors should be free of clerical and administrative duties and should direct their major attention to working directly with and for students."

These recommendations have not been fulfilled. They are considered financially impractical. Many schools do not have one counselor for every 500 students, let alone one for every 50. And some counselors have extensive clerical and administrative duties that make it impossible for most of their time to be spent directly on "the worth and well-being of the students."

Look at the situation in your own school. See what is available and utilize it. But realize that the special psychological training your counselors may have had does not increase the number of hours in the day. Again, counselors are *people*, imperfect and limited in many cases by the other things they are required to do.

Recognizing the load, try to resist scapegoating the counselor for your frustration when the door is closed because someone else is in there, or even when he or she has escaped for a coffee break with the teachers. (Chances are that during the break the counselor finds himself using the time to get through to Mrs. Gilbert about some kid not cutting math, or a similar problem.) If the counselor is busy, make an appointment, leave a sealed note, or come back another time.

Almost any kind of problem can be taken to school counselors because almost any kind of problem influences how you act and how well you are able to learn in school. If your concern is beyond the counselor's power to help, you may expect to be told this and to receive suggestions as to where help might be available.

Counselors commonly provide information and answers to questions. But just as commonly, counselors listen and allow you to talk, and this turns out to be one of the greatest learning experiences of all. Being allowed to talk in a confidential setting with a person interested in you and accepting of what you have to say can be a giant step in learning about yourself. It may be a new experience to be able to talk freely, not to have to be afraid of the rejection of the people around you for slipping and saying what you really want to say, or for being a little emotional in your expressions.

Chapter Nine

THE EMOTIONAL COMPONENT

"I never laughed so much before in my life. Everybody was having a good time. Then things got a little wild, you could say. Things went a little too far. Somebody got mad. And things got out of hand. It was awful."

Another time, another girl; "It was the most exciting evening ever. The music and the lights were fantastic. Everyone was out to have fun, you know. But nobody was out to mess things up. No hassles."

And another; "David. Oh, David, the way my heart is pounding. Just to touch. Oh, David. Do kiss me."

As always, it is impossible to adequately communicate and define the emotional component in fun. We can only hint at it and theorize. But we come closer to understanding, maybe knock loose a few false ideas, from the exercise, and it is worth the try.

"The more emotional, the more fun," I have heard said. And surely, emotions have to do with the intensity of our experiences. Emotions are feelings. So you could say, "The more fun feelings, the more fun feelings" to mean almost the same as "The more emotional, the more fun." But then you would be left with the other side of the coin: "The more unhappy feelings, the more unhappy feelings."

The point is, not just any and every emotional experience contributes to fun. Some can slam you into circumstances with very unhappy consequences.

Why Emotions?

Emotions are the feelings associated with the most significant moments in our lives, moments when it seems imperative to act and fulfill some urgent need. Emotions serve us at the most basic levels —survival and procreation; that is, the continuation of the human race. Without emotions, we would not exist. Our ancestors would have died off.

Emotions are states of feeling that are accompanied by characteristic *motor and glandular activities*. Theorists disagree as to which comes first, the feeling or the changes in the body. But without debate, emotions involve more than neural activity or feelings; there are a number of distinct and rapid changes in the body during emotional states. These changes prepare us for possible associated physical activity.

In prehistoric times, anger meant *attack, strike, hurt, kill*. Fear meant *run, retreat, escape, hide*. Sexual arousal meant *seek direct physical release* in a manner that would conceive offspring, regardless of whether the purpose of this activity was known or not.

With the oncoming of civilization and man's desire to have a better life than animalistic packs could provide, many complex procedures were developed and refined for the satisfaction of the basic needs. And many new needs have been created within us through the learning experiences of our highly organized and systematized world. The more stable and intelligent among us work within the developing system and ever-changing establishment to make things better for everyone.

In the complicated business of trying to preserve individual rights and living together in peace and mutual benefit, the base responses of our cave-dwelling ancestors have become irrational and punishable by the people through our governments. Raw emotional urgings now seldom point the way to satisfaction, but instead intensify further dissatisfaction.

Bare aggression as a response to anger and frustration is not satisfying in the long run, as we have noted in consideration of the *frustration-aggression cycle*. Except in cases where the jungle has been thrust suddenly upon us and we must literally fight to survive, bare aggression is defeating because it brings further frustration.

Growing up has changed from learning to be an effective hunter or fire-tender to learning to channel emotional drive into acceptable, productive activity. Nevertheless, the basic feelings are still with us.

Sometimes we experience them openly and honestly. Sometimes, because of the guilt or unacceptability we may associate with them, we repress them deep within the unconscious. But they remain, at times prodding us toward the animalistic.

Of course, there are moments when it is vital that we follow our impulses. If we step off a curb and see a car bearing down on us, we would be smart to do what comes naturally and jump back out of the way. In other moments it is not wise to follow impulses. If the teacher passes out a surprise exam, we may feel like running away or daydreaming, but we would be wiser to face up to the situation and do the best we can. In any event, it is no fun to keep emotions bottled up without expression. It can even be downright dangerous.

Consider a more realistic fantasy, if you will: imagine yourself angry at all the people who have authority over you. Imagine constant unfairness. Imagine forces that keep you from accomplishing all the good work you try to do. Imagine yourself in a life-style that does not permit you to have much physical exercise. And imagine having beliefs that make you feel guilty for having angry impulses or even daydreams of vengeance. There are many people in real-life situations such as this.

Stomach ulcers furnish just one common example of the consequences of prolonged emotional stress. When a person is angry, sometimes unconsciously, for long periods without adequate expression, his stomach secretes an abundance of acid that can literally eat holes in him.

What's Going On?

Mysteries are everywhere in the world of emotion. It is a world that is sometimes beautiful, spooky, exotic, and depressing. Sincerity is often in question. Does this person really feel what he seems to feel or am I just being led along? Is he really mad or just playing games? Does she really think the jokes are that funny or is she just being nice? Is he pleased or disappointed with the hand he is holding? (The word "hand" applies to cards and/or romance.)

It is hard to know for sure what emotion another person is experiencing. It is even hard to know for sure what emotion you may be experiencing yourself. And this complicates things.

Have you ever heard of a polygraph? You may know it best as a lie detector. Its function is to guess whether or not a person is telling the truth by measuring physiological reactions that are expected to accompany anger or fear. There are several versions of the machine but most commonly it involves measurements of blood pressure, breathing, and sweat gland activity. The rationale for its use rests on the assumption that such physiological changes are beyond a person's conscious control. Although a person might be able to control bodily movements and facial expressions, it is assumed that reactions under the control of the autonomic nervous system are beyond conscious control.

Questions are asked the subject while trained experts make predictions as to whether or not the answers are true based on the degree of emotion the machine suggests is being experienced. But as the experts will tell you, the content of some questions can cause emotional responses even when the subject tells the truth. It is a tricky procedure and can be misleading.

Emotions can be aroused within a person without his or her awareness on the conscious level. Carl Rogers, a noted psychotherapist, once suggested a fundamental concept which he termed *congruence*. He suggested that emotion might be seen as operating at three different levels: *experience*, *awareness*, and *communication*. In different people, and in the same people at different times, the degree to which these three levels coincide and are *congruent* with one another will differ.

Emotions experienced on the physiological level are not always known on the awareness level. We do not always communicate and share emotions we are personally aware of with those around us. And we have reasons, sound or faulty, for this lack of congruency.

Alan, for example, is a proud young track star who fails to clear the fence he was trying to jump while some girls he knows are watching.

"Like Captain America," says his buddy, as he runs up beside him. "What a spill. You all right?"

"Forget it," says Alan sharply.

"Don't get mad at me," objects his friend. "I didn't raise that fence on you."

"I'm not mad. Just hurt my knee a little." Alan hobbles away.

Alan may not know he is angry. It may be unacceptable for him to see that he is mad. He may be blocking his total frustration from his awareness. Then again, he may well be aware that he is thoroughly angry, but just may not want to communicate the fact to anyone else. There are many times, often with good reason, when we are not congruent.

A girl fully aware of how bored she is at a friend's party, for example, would have good reason for not communicating her anger at having given up a wanted date to attend. She might be very disappointed but still not want to hurt her friend's feelings. There is no shame in not being emotionally congruent all the time. But it can keep a person from thoroughly enjoying life.

On the other hand, the girl's trouble may stem from her not being her true self. The got-to-be-me approach comes out in different ways. Translated destructively by a few, it proclaims, I'm going to do what I feel like doing no matter who is hurt. But, of course, with more productive shadings, this approach is supported throughout the book.

In considerations of congruence, it is all too easy to short-circuit logic and overemphasize the need for immediate emotional expression at the expense of future opportunities for more pleasurable emotional experiences. An intelligent, life-long view calls for congruence in more than experience, awareness, and communication of emotions. Congruence also is needed for our values, logic, and actions throughout life.

What Is Laughter?

Most of us would agree that laughter is the criteria of whether or not a joke is funny. At least it is the criteria of whether or not it is funny to a given person at a given time and place. Of course, this given person may have heard the story before. He might still believe the story is funny but not laugh because the surprise element is missing. The punch line has to come suddenly, with little or no warning, for it to be laughably funny. Then, too, this person might feel like laughing but manage to keep himself under control.

What is laughter? It is an emotional experience associated with fun and good times. It is a kind of emotional explosion, a physical earthquake.

Laughter is not all the same. There are as many different types of laughter as there are different types of people, different types of situations prompting laughter, and different combinations of the two. Included in the spectrum are those sudden bursts of open joy, the ones that come as products of the other components of the suggested formula for fun. *Action*, for example, can provoke laughter. Visualize a dozen people, almost any age, racing up a hill in the park together —laughing. *Discovery*—a boy finally catching on to a tricky solid geometry problem, or a girls' basketball team suddenly bringing together a new play—can cause laughter. So can *belonging*. Think of a girl and boy, in love, embracing after being separated a few days— laughing. Laughter often goes with peak moments in fun experiences.

People sometimes laugh because things are going well and they are happy. Much more mysterious is the laughter that goes with or comes out of humor. Think of the last few jokes you have heard. Why would you have sudden bursts of joy about them?

"Well, they were just funny," you might answer.

And I might ask, "Oh? Why was that? What was so funny? What made you feel so good all of a sudden that you would laugh?"

Everyone has hidden feelings and urges to do things that we would never let ourselves do. Most of us would not let ourselves do at least some of the things we have imagined or felt like doing. Also, deep down in most of us there are things of which we are ashamed, things we have done or thought that are so awful—so much in conflict with the self we want to be—that we have not spoken of them even with our most trusted friends. There are things so unacceptable and uncomfortable to think about that we hide them even from our own conscious knowledge through *repression*. Still, the emotions from these threatening feelings and urges are present and active, sometimes building up tremendous tension.

Emotional expression through laughter releases and eases tension. In ways differing somewhat from person to person, humor has a wonderful way of letting the unbearable become laughable and helping us cope with forbidden fears and urges.

Most of us give way and laugh at frightening things, when we are far enough removed from them not to be experiencing serious fear and dread. Spooky movies bring more laughs than cries of terror.

We laugh at the important. Pulling people down from their pedestals, through humor, has always seemed good sport, unless we identify with the particular hero, idol, or leader in a way that brings us down with the same blow.

We laugh at things related to sex. All of us have repressed things related to our elimination functions, our sex organs, and our urges to perform forbidden acts. Some repressions occurred long ago as a consequence of no-no's emotionally imposed by grown-ups when we were children. Hidden within the unconscious, unable to be brushed away with mature logic, they continue to exert irrational pressure that can be triggered over and over again through humor.

We laugh at the mistakes people make. Sophisticated people laugh at the more complex errors of intelligent people. Dull and immature people laugh at almost any mistake or failing, even those of retarded, helpless, or crippled people. We all have deep feelings about not being quite as capable as we want to be. We have all made mistakes of which we have been ashamed. And seeing someone else foul up and appear even more foolish than we feel can often plunge us into sudden bursts of laughter.

Of course, part of developing emotional maturity is learning to keep expressions of emotion under control. No one enjoys being ridiculed through laughter. It nearly always hurts the self-picture and causes bad feelings. Some laughter—but, obviously, not all—is inappropriate and destructive.

One of the signs of a person's mental health is a sense of humor. And a sense of humor is one of the best tools in maintaining good mental health. Our ability to have fun and enjoy a full and healthy life often depends on that sense of humor—the ability not only to laugh at wit and to see humor in the world around us, but the ability to laugh at our own troubles, superficially and in depth.

Cry, Express, Work

What's so bad about crying a little? When you feel like it, crying may be a very good thing to do. It might even be fun, under the right circumstances. The release of tension it provides could be very beneficial.

But crying often disturbs the people around us, causing additional complications and frustrations which defeat the purpose. One of the problems with crying is its association with sadness much more than with joy. Crying is culturally defined as a plea for help and an indication of sorrow. It conveys distress. It is even seen as a sign of inferiority and weakness. As a result, crying must be used with discretion and in relative privacy.

Many other emotional outlets are readily available, especially to those people who go along with the first two fun components listed in the formula—*action* and *discovery*. Vigorous physical activity is a healthy method of releasing tension and expressing emotions. As noted earlier, most of our emotions are closely related to the preparation of the body for action. Exercise, sports, bikeriding, running, walking, hiking, swimming, dancing, and physical labor can all provide substitute activity that helps satisfy our basic needs.

Beyond the more vigorous releases, many sublimations and expressions through the arts are available. The long list of possible opportunities includes painting, woodworking, weaving, dramatics, singing (alone or with many), debating, religious worship, writing (stories, letters, poetry, anything on how you feel), cheering at games and rallies, rapping with friends, political activity, social work, teaching things to others that are important to you, patriotic observances, reading stories with which you can identify, and talking about your personal concerns with people who are accepting of your point of view.

The key to civilized survival is to discover contributing life-styles that get along with the rest of the world, that help support the group effort which sustains us but include regular fulfilling outlets to satisfy emotion at the same time. The goal is difficult to achieve at times, but we need to find ways to enjoy emotions, not suffer from them.

Chapter Ten

BELONGING MEANS MANY THINGS

George sat near me on the bleachers for a while at the after-school dance. Then he got up and strode out onto the floor. Moving through the crowd, he paused to stand with one cluster, then another. Few, if any, students returned his smile. No one spoke more than to return his quiet "Hi." He danced one dance, with a girl whose distant gaze conveyed that she was somewhere else. Alone, he stood by the far door for a few minutes. And shrugging to himself, he left. It's no fun when you feel you don't belong.

I learned later that after the dance George met some other kids who accepted him. But they were kids he had been trying to stay away from, with whom he had been doing things he really did not want to do. And it was this afternoon that they got caught. The need to be accepted and belong can affect our well-being in many ways and for many reasons.

The Need to Belong

This pervasive force in our lives is apparent at all levels of the *hierarchy of needs*, outlined in Chapter Three. Meeting our most basic *biological* and *safety* needs demands the tolerance and the co-operation of other people. A reasonable measure of belonging at these basic levels is necessary for the continuation of life. *Love* and *esteem* are based in the caring, warmth, and interacting friendship of those around us. During the teen years, most of our needs to belong are in these two areas. And throughout our lives, it is here that we most frequently associate the concept of belonging. Finally, *self-*

actualization requires the acceptance of people in unique and special ways. An author, for example, who attempts to actualize through great writing cannot reach his goal without the acceptance of his readers. We need to belong in one way or another regardless of where we may be trying to exist within the hierarchy. We feel this deeply at all levels.

Throughout history we have had the need to belong, along with the other side of the same coin—the fear of rejection. In centuries past, for example, our ancestors lived in tribal settings where absolute loyalty was demanded by the group. The members of the tribe were bound closely together by common goals and by customs, mores, and folkways which everyone was expected to follow. To go against the apparent will of the group in such primitive settings meant a very real threat to survival. Within the tribe there was food, shelter, warmth, and protection from enemies. But those who failed to belong were very likely to be thrust into the jungle to fend for themselves. And those who violated the taboos or sacred rules were often put to death.

Much the same can be said of the later feudal systems and of the totalitarian systems of today. Even in our country, where individual freedom has developed to the greatest extent the world has ever known, group pressures are dynamics of daily life. All societies, governments, communes, and families maintain requirements of membership. And the consequences of not belonging and of being rejected for failure to meet these requirements continue to be severe.

Of course, problems of group membership have grown more complex. We no longer belong to one single group but to many—groups having strict rules that are well-defined, groups whose membership requirements are hazy and changing with the moment, and groups which are in distinct conflict with one another. Nevertheless, with our long heritage of group living, it is not at all surprising that we should feel a life-or-death pressure to belong to and go along with the crowd, whichever crowd we may find ourselves in at the moment.

Belonging—Right or Wrong?

The evening had been fun, so far. And she liked Mike much more than she thought she could like anyone on a first date. She liked the way he wore his hair. And the idea of a boy a few years older than she was held fascination. It was exciting all around.

But suddenly, Anne was worried. Mike had turned off onto a dark side road. Now he was pulling into a grove of trees and stopping the car. For long seconds there was only darkness, and it was quiet except for Lucy and her date in the back seat. Anne knew she was in over her head.

Mike flicked on the dash lights, reached down under the seat, and brought up a bottle. "The party begins," he announced.

"Yeah!" the other boy shouted from behind them.

"Ladies first," said Mike, and handed the bottle to Anne.

"I'd better not. I really don't like it."

Mike pushed the bottle at her chin.

"No kidding," she said. "My folks would kill me if they knew I was even in a car with the stuff."

"What's wrong with drinking? It's legal, almost," Lucy laughed. "Who's going to tell your folks? Me, maybe?"

Anne managed a swallow or two. It burned the full length of her throat. She knew this was only the beginning. She knew she would be expected to drink more and wondered what else would be expected of her.

Actually, she would not have come in the first place if Lucy had not pressured her. She wished she had not lied about spending the night with Lucy to do homework.

Now they were passing a purple cigarette around. It smelled like burning rope.

"This you got to go with," Lucy told her, and inhaled deeply. "Everybody, but everybody, is into this."

Anne felt sick to her stomach and wished she could somehow turn back the clock.

We all want to belong. We want the acceptance of the people around us, and we want the affection of at least a few individuals. These are vital needs. At times nothing else may seem so important, in spite of the guilt feelings and dangers which may follow afterward. This is very natural and basic in human life.

We *know* this is true on a rational, intellectual level because we can see the need to get along as it affects those around us in our world of work and play. Also, we *feel* it is true on a deep emotional level that is rooted in our earliest childhood experiences and in the centuries of man's dependence on others in the development of organized society.

The Pressures of the Crowd

"Come on. Everybody's doing it." You have probably heard this more than once, or maybe you have said it yourself. "I mean, when everybody's doing it, you go along, whether you really want to or not. If you don't, you're out of it. And then you are nowhere. Right?"

What do you think? Nowhere? Maybe it depends.

The need to go along with the crowd causes overwhelming feelings. The fear of rejection can be powerful. It is healthy and wise to be sensitive to the wishes of those around us. If we are doing things offensive to the group, we had better look in the mirror, check armpits, and consider the possibility of change. But the old *everybody's doing it* is a poor excuse for doing anything. Just because the *rest of the crowd* seems to be doing something is not proof positive that it is the best thing for us to do.

Of course, to begin with, "everybody" is a phony term. Seldom, if ever, is there a time when *everybody* is doing it. And when the rest of the crowd is actually doing something, the possibility is always present that many individuals in the crowd do not want to be doing what they are doing.

When we feel pressure from the crowd to do something we do not feel quite right about, chances are that there are others who feel as we do. It may be time to speak up. We are the crowd as much as anyone else. We, as individuals, can exert pressure by asserting our own points of view. What we say when we speak up is likely to be interpreted by others as the pressure of the crowd. And it is. People belong to us as much as we belong to them.

In coping with any pressure of the crowd, remember that we have at least three general choices of action: we can go along with the crowd; try to change the crowd and get its members to go along with us; or find a new crowd.

Such decisions are difficult to make. And when ambivalence seems to make deciding impossible, it may be time to turn our thoughts to the larger crowd to which we belong. What would the people we respect most in our family, our school, and our community want us to do. And if we hold religious beliefs, what do these tell us to do? To be in conflict with other people we care about or with the meaningful values of the self can be painfully destructive.

On Making Friends

Happily, most of us arrive on this earth with at least one or two people close to us who let us know that we belong. We do not have to earn family membership. There are those who usually care for us no matter what we do. The few unfortunates for whom this is not true are destined to have difficult problems in this area. The deep-rooted feelings they hold can keep telling them that they do not belong, guiding them to act as though they don't, promoting a self-fulfilling prophecy.

No matter what their reason for this attitude, people who go around acting as though no one likes them have a hard time making friends. "I can't make friends," some will tell you. "Who'd like me? I never make a good impression. No looks. And I can't do anything well. I mean, I'm no good in sports. Can't play a guitar or anything. Summer comes and I can't even work up a tan. Dead end." Attitudes create "born losers."

Regardless of our feelings, and regardless of whether we want just one friend or many, we can improve our chances through a realistic understanding of what friendship is all about.

One more obvious idea is the importance of making a good impression on the person or persons we want to accept us as friends. But some try hard at this without success. One very common mistake is to try to impress people by appearance, talent, property, or status. "Hey, my hair looks like that new superstar," or "Lucky you, to get to dance with handsome me," some communicate through manner and appearance. "Did you see in the last half when I got the ball?" or "I'm going to turn up the amps and play a little something I made up myself," or "I'm a big man around here," some others might say. And all of this might pay off. But it might not. An over-emphasis on such things can prevent us from making friends—certainly, from making close friends.

Very often, teen needs are in the esteem area. A sincere compliment nearly always helps more than calling attention to your own good features or accomplishments. We usually have our best luck in making friends when we focus our attention on other people and their feelings. Making a grand impression on people and making friends of them are two different things.

This does not mean we should pretend to be less than we are. Playing the role of something we are not is a dishonesty which is sure to backfire. Also, a person should be able to relax and be himself, especially with his friends.

One of the most important factors in *close* friendships has been found to be *mutual satisfaction of needs*. Note the word *mutual*. There should be a balanced flow of give and take. In any genuine friendship, both sides must keep this in mind. There should be giving *and* receiving on both sides.

Of course, the needs of people differ somewhat from person to person. And as a result, different personalities appeal to different personalities. Some people take to each other, and some people do not. There are some people we may never win as friends. And there are some who may never win us as friends, no matter how hard they try. But our chances of gaining friends are always enhanced when we are able to focus on other people and try to understand their needs.

We come to belong when we answer the needs of the people around us, and when that beautiful thing happens, they in turn have the active desire to answer our needs.

Understanding can improve the odds for success. But, good friend, sometimes all you can do is try. And if understanding does not work, then with a touch of pity for those who missed being your friend, move on and try somewhere else. By all means, do not compromise yourself in an attempt to belong. A very important acceptance in our lives is from within. We can suffer the rejection of others with less pain and complication than the personal self-rejection that comes when we violate our own taboos.

Chapter Eleven

YOUR VOICE IN WHAT TO DO
AND BE

"Ain't nobody going to tell me what to do," said the boy, jabbing a black strand of hair back from his angry face. "People always pushing me around. Sure, I hit him." From the room outside my door came the sound of the other boy throwing up in the wastebasket.

"I have to tell them over there," the teacher who brought him to me had said moments before, motioning toward the principal's office. "But maybe you could talk with him first. He'll get himself thrown out of here, the mood he's in."

"What happened, Len?" I asked the boy. "I thought things were going better for you."

"Nothing," he answered.

"Hank tells me you two just came around a corner and bumped into each other."

"He got in my way."

"Just got in your way."

"He didn't do nothing. I shouldn't have hit him," Len told me. "Just nobody going to push me around anymore. I'm always getting pushed. My father, the teachers, everybody keeps telling me what to do. Folks don't let me do what I want to do. 'You get in trouble if you run with those kids,' they tell me. 'Get home by ten.' And last night the car with the red lights pulls up and says, 'What you doing on the street this time of night, boy?' And they call my folks, and my folks say, 'Told you. Now you're in trouble, running around at all hours.' "

In a variety of ways, we all want a voice in deciding our own destiny and in deciding what we will do. We want to have a voice in deciding the sort of fun to have. Basically, we want to do what we feel like doing. But feelings and impulses do not always lead to fun in the long run. We all have urges that can be downright destructive. And life is not going to be much fun until we know how much voice we can expect to have, why we cannot have it all our way, how the other person's voice is also important, and how to keep freedom alive so that all voices can be heard and influence what is to be.

Of course, while scapegoating and making immature demands are sadly destructive, speaking out with intelligence can be productive. It can be a healthy release. It can guide group action into constructive channels. It can be stimulating exercise in thinking things through with others. Asserting yourself, intelligently, at the right time and place can save the day. Your chances for success and happiness depend on your capacity to act on what you see is right for you rather than just going along.

"I've had it up to here with this character," one boy related. "He makes out there's something wrong with you if you don't see it all his way. He calls you chicken if you don't go along with him. I figured most of the guys thought the way he did. Most of them chimed in with whatever he said. They sounded as if they wanted to let everybody know they were just as tough as he was.

"But Friday night was the last straw. This joker says we're going to rip off tires. I looked around and didn't see anyone who was about to disagree with him. I figured if these guys were going to keep on like this, I was through. I was having more fun in Explorers anyway, especially with this Canoe Base trip we have coming up, with girls no less. I'd drop this bunch. This guy is bigger than I am, but I was mad.

"'I really think you got a loose screw,' I told him. 'I've had it, boy! It isn't bad enough you waste our time with all those stupid, do-nothing ideas of yours. Now, you want to get us thrown in jail.'

"Then, the craziest thing happened. Even the guys who usually talked up his ideas threw in behind *me*. The whole gang seemed to turn on him. Oh, there were some who still didn't say anything. I guess you can never tell where some guys stand. They just follow along.

"Well, this character wrinkled up his face like he wanted to fight at first, but after he saw how things were going he tried to laugh it off, telling us he really didn't want to steal any tires. He just wanted to see what we would do. That's what he said, anyway."

It is not always simple to find out what the crowd actually expects of you. What the majority of the crowd wants and what a couple of loudmouths say the crowd wants may turn out to be quite different things. If you stand up for what you think is right and refuse to go against your better judgment, you often discover you are not alone. The odds are in favor of there being others in the crowd who feel as you do. They may just be waiting and hoping for such an opportunity, needing someone brave enough to express their point of view.

When Backing Down Is Not Backing Down

Dealing with the pressures of the crowd is largely a matter of facing facts. And one fact you must face eventually is the true character of the groups to which you belong. In the real sense of the word, you cannot *belong* to groups that are in serious conflict with what you know is right.

The logic is plain and true: know your groups—what you can and cannot do if you are to belong. And know yourself—that is, know your *self*. If you cannot do what you know you should and remain in the group, play it smart. If you are so dominated that you are not allowed to be yourself, it is time to leave. Most of all, be yourself. Do not be forced to do what you do not want to do just because of name-calling, or the like.

Of course, only you can decide how you want to play it. You may silently withdraw. Or you may try to change the group. You may want to fight fire with fire. "It takes one to know one," you might say. Or you might raise the question, "Just who is chicken, anyway?" You may try to expose the name-callers for what they are. But if things have gone so far that this does not work, get out before you get in any deeper.

Whatever you do, do not let yourself get into a situation where you cannot control what happens to you. Keep your eyes open to dangers to life and limb. Do not be so foolish, for example, as to get into cars with people you do not know well enough to trust. Do not become isolated from those you may need to ask for help. And remember, always, there is a point at which the brave retreat. It may not be easy to turn and walk away. It may take much more courage than following along. But it often pays off in the long run.

The crowd is *you* as much as it is anyone else. Your own intelligent thought and action can do much to make the pressures of the crowd be what you know they ought to be. At the same time, remember that the method is part of the message. And guaranteeing the other person's right to a recognized point of view is the most effective route in guaranteeing your own.

Other Points of View

There is a story about two men who were talking to each other on walkie-talkies and fell into an argument. One man was on a tall mountain; the other, in a valley. The argument was over the position of a fire on a hill in between. One of the men said it was *"up* there." The other insisted it was *"down* there."

Now we know that these men must not have been very bright. From where we sit, it is obvious that neither of the men was completely right or completely wrong. They were merely viewing the fire from different points of view. And all that was needed for them to resolve their differences and get on with the important business of putting out the fire was for each to recognize the other man's point of view.

It is difficult to imagine such a ridiculous situation or two men being this stupid and childish. But much of the time there are situations just as ridiculous around us—situations where people remain blinded to all but their own points of view.

The boy ruining an afternoon date with a girl because he does not take her wishes into consideration, a girl angry with her parents because of the restrictions they have placed on her, a student who thinks the teacher does not like him because she gets after him are examples of not focusing on other points of view. The resulting false impressions hurt everyone concerned.

If we are to know the truth of things, we must keep an open mind to other points of view. This does not mean we should drastically change our opinions with each new point of view we hear expressed. This will happen at times. But more often, the other points of view will supplement and increase our understanding of what we already know. It takes more than one eye to view things in perspective.

Understanding Parents

"I mean, I can understand my mother," a girl told me in a small group discussion the other day. "But she can't understand me. Like, she just goes deaf when I tell her I'm going to be all right just walking a few blocks down the street by myself at night. Then, she wants to tell me how it was way back when she was a girl."

"Yeah," said someone else, "my dad always comes in with, 'When I was a boy . . .' "

"Things are different now," another said, and it went on like this for a while, everyone taking a turn at putting down their parents because they talked about a world of twenty or thirty years ago when they were kids.

Then they turned to me as though they expected me to square off with them and try to put them down in defense of all the parents of the world. "I could tell you, of course, how your parents have your best interests at heart," I told them. "And I could suggest that maybe people, even parents, learn a little something as they live on through the years. But I think you know all that. What I do want to put to you is the question of how you plan to do a better job.

"Now, I know from having listened to you that you are working through a lot of problems. Some of you said you wished that you had had more help in heading off some of the painful things that have happened to you. What do you do," I asked them, "in a few years from now if you have kids of your own and you start to see them having some of the same problems that you went through? I mean, the bodies they will be walking around in will be much the same as the ones you are wearing today. Love and hate will give them much the same sensations. And if you are any kind of a parent, you will look at what is going on and think, 'I know what is happening, and I want to help. I want to prevent the hurt I know can come.'

"They will think you don't understand, and you will tell them of your own experiences, how you felt, and what happened. Then some of them will listen and learn, but some of them will shut you out and think, 'What do you know, with all that junk that happened back when kids were still driving cars, hair was still in, and skirts were up to here?'

"So, suppose there is something you don't want your kids to do, like jet-kiting when they haven't even been licensed, and they turn you off. What do you do? How are you going to do a better job of keeping your cool and doing what you know you have to do than your parents now do with you?"

For those who want to be fair, these are things to think about. The manner in which the developing person asserts his voice in the family and the response of the parents in each instance determines not just what the person will do but what he will be.

It is not just today that parents want to get along with their youngsters. Tomorrow, ten years from now, they will want to get along. They will want to experience the respect that comes later when kids look back and say, "Thanks for caring enough to do what you thought was best in spite of the hassle."

Lee Ann talked her parents into going to a show instead of being in the house when she had her party. A carload of uninvited boys from across town crashed the party. The invited guests managed to repel the invasion, but not before the party had turned into a bloody brawl.

It's hard to imagine that anything could go wrong until after things have gone wrong.

A number of years ago I gave a talk to a High Y group—a bold and frank discussion of boy-girl relations, with me the only male present. One sincere question asked was, "How can we convince our parents that we are old enough to take care of ourselves? How do we convince them that nothing is going to happen?" My answer had to be that they could not convince them. There really are dangers and risks in this world.

A year later, one of the girls in that group was killed, beaten beyond recognition, in her own home by a boy from her class in school.

Parents are more justly concerned than is sometimes understood. Teens should certainly have a voice in their own affairs, but this does not mean adults should be excluded from their good times. Adults can help guarantee this voice.

Chapter Twelve

BEING SOMEBODY

A boy transfers into a school from out-of-town. He has been in trouble and really wants a fresh start. The main office personnel keeps the secret. Yet, after a few short days or less, he begins telling it around that he had a big drug problem, ripped off three cars, is on probation, or the like.

Where is the sense to it?

In having to be somebody. The need is compelling.

Similarly, I have known of cases where a girl suffered a publicized rape and was transferred to a distant school where no one knew her. Then, again, the word gets around because the girl is sharing the secret of which she is honestly ashamed, confiding in people she hardly knows.

Again, the need to be somebody is compelling.

Somebody—What and How?

"What I am," a girl once told me, "is a dandelion amongst roses."

What is being somebody?

For people nearly starving, trapped in a cave-in, or falling from 10,000 feet with a bad chute, the all-consuming challenge is to live through the current crisis. Applying the hierarchy of needs, the most urgent need can be to simply manage to be *somebody alive*.

But for those of us thinking about the subject while writing or reading a book and functioning beyond the basic biological and safety needs levels, the answer lies within a more highly developed self. The judgment and the feeling of whether we are somebody depends on the contents of the self and the value placed on the things with which we identify.

People are different in this respect. For some it is enough to belong. For some it can be quite enough to be loved by one alone. For others, clearly, this is not enough. They must have widely recognized accomplishments, popularity, leadership opportunities, and power.

How does a person get to be somebody in this world? Some try retreating to childhood—back into the time when others took care of us, when we had no major responsibilities, when others thought for us, rewarding us when we were nice and punishing us when we were naughty. Of course, teenagers who do this usually dissociate and try not to admit they are doing it. But they are easy to spot because they never assume responsibility for themselves. Their power seems only in receiving and taking from others, never helping.

Some people create identities that gather recognition. They join causes that will accept them. They reach out to belong to groups with which they can emotionally identify. Not all such identities and identifications are positive and constructive, but not all are negative and destructive, either. Most have extensive rationalizations to support their total worth.

Some people identify with the future and find meaning in sublimating their energies into the long, complex preparation for responsible citizenship.

Often, with different moods and circumstances, teens take turns at regressing, forming temporary identities, and identifying with their goals for the future. But through it all, being somebody is largely a matter of self-picture. In this, a dynamic blending occurs that stresses interdependencies.

In order to be somebody and gain recognition, you must feel that you are of worth to others. But more important, you need to feel of worth to yourself, that is, to your *self*—including all the people you care about, the people who are a part of your self. You need to be somebody of worth to your total self. And to feel worthy, you must avoid doing things that you believe to be unworthy.

It becomes difficult to be at peace with yourself when you act in conflict with the beliefs and standards of the people you care about, even when their beliefs and standards are not your own. "I don't want to go against what my parents have planned for me all these years." You have probably heard this statement every day, in one manner or another. "But the kids I have been with this year are not going that way. And, me, I think there's a crying need for this other thing. Maybe it doesn't pay as much, but I see it as more important. Still, it really bothers me that I am disappointing my parents. Maybe, I'll feel differently tomorrow."

Identity during the teens is hard to stabilize. The constantly changing body needs and appearance make it almost impossible since the somebody we can be and want to be is not the same from day to day. New experiences and even physical growth and development can alter needs and values. Even the setting in which we find ourselves can call for a new somebody. A somebody in one place is not necessarily a somebody in another place and time.

"I was really somebody," a boy in Washington, D.C., told me. "Money was coming in like you wouldn't believe. I was selling stuff —like playing God, you know. And then I met this girl. And wow, the stars and sky and everything I ever wanted but never knew I wanted, you know. But her mother wouldn't let her have anything to do with me. And big man was nothing. Nothing." It is not only today's self we have to get along with, but also tomorrow's.

Been Cut Down Lately?

When was the last time someone called you a belittling or obscene name? It is a common problem we all have to cope with if we are to maintain a somebody self. How did you react?

Unfortunately, a great many people react only to the momentary impact of the words. They do not understand what is really going on beneath the surface. Their reactions seldom prove anything in the long run, and may actually accomplish the opposite of what they set out to do.

When insulting names are flying, a distorted sense of "self-respect" seems to dominate the moment. At school, name-calling may be used to keep someone from reporting a violation of a rule. On the street, it may be used to force teenagers into acts of vandalism. At parties, it may be used to bring pressure on those not going along with the crowd, regardless of where the crowd seems to be going. On the highway, it may be used to stimulate any one of a number of deadly ventures.

Some people actually stay away from fun activities and adventurous good times for fear of being called names. Some teens are so afraid of being called names that they let down in schoolwork. They avoid being helpful. They resist doing useful work where name-callers might see them. They seriously hurt themselves and undermine the well-being of their community and their country.

There is one particularly good defense that can make you immune to name-calling. It is your *understanding*, your knowledge of just what is going on when someone starts calling you names. Once you really understand, you will find it much easier to deal intelligently with the problems as they arise. But first you need to know the answers to a few questions. Why are so many of us such pushovers for the threat of being called names? Why should anyone want to call other people names in the first place?

Most of the answers lie in an understanding of the self and the discussions of self-defense found earlier in this book.

Some Need to Pull Others Down

Insecure and confused youngsters call others "chicken" to compensate for their own feelings of cowardice and inferiority. They get a lift out of pulling down those who have greater ability or character. They feel they must constantly confirm their worth by proving themselves "better," or more daring, than someone else. By insinuation and name-calling, and in some cases, by acts of bravado, they attempt to compensate for their inability to live normal, wholesome lives. They feel courageous by comparison with those who "backed down." It does not matter whether the thing they want done is courageous or cowardly. The situation is twisted so that no matter what you do you are called "chicken."

Larry was one of those who call "chicken." He was short for his age. He had never done well in school. And there were those who said he usually looked and smelled as though he needed to wash. None of these things in themselves made him a typical "chicken-caller." It was his attitude. Most of the kids who knew him would tell you, "Larry is always looking for trouble."

On his way to school, for example, he often tried to talk those he was with into skipping for the day. If they would not cut school, he called them "chicken." If they did, he would dream up something else, like throwing rocks at street lights, sniffing glue, or shoplifting at a local store. And whenever they did not go along with his ideas, he called them "chicken."

He needed help in understanding his problems, but he would not accept it, even when it was offered. He felt uncomfortable looking squarely at his problems, so he merely continued to try to run away from them. Larry was headed for serious trouble, and he was taking anyone who could not stand being called "chicken" along with him.

Chicken Calls "Chicken"

Similar to the person who constantly feels he must pull others down is the one who defends his shabby self through the mechanism called *projection*. In fact, the two types may be one and the same, but with different emphases. In projection, you will recall, a person attributes his undesirable traits to other people. And the situation is further complicated by the fact that he may be completely unaware of doing it.

When there are things about a person that do not fit into his self-picture, he may be unable to admit these flaws in himself but only be able to project them onto others. What he feels deep down inside, he imagines he sees in those around him.

If he is afraid that he is cowardly, he may not be able to admit this to himself. In defense of his self-picture, he may see *projected* cowardly streaks in others. If he finds it difficult to be loyal to his friends, he may imagine that his friends are disloyal to him. He may even go so far as to imagine that they are plotting against him. The more unworthy he feels, the more he may need to see unworthiness in those about him.

Something Important to Remember

If people call you names, it is because of something that is inside of them, not inside of you. Take the focus of your attention off yourself and put it on the name-callers, where it belongs. Look beneath the surface at their motives. You will see that they act the way they do because of something they feel in themselves, not because of what they really see in someone else.

Losing self-respect because you are being called names is dangerous as well as faulty thinking. What you think of yourself should be well enough founded that it can resist mere name-calling. If it is not, you will have bad times ahead.

Chapter Thirteen

THE LOOK AHEAD

"Where is it all going?" "What's ahead?" The question comes one way or another, eventually. And the answer better be one we want to hear; whether we are speaking of a date, job, school, a new relationship between people, or the whole of life. If we have nothing good to look forward to, if what we have been doing leads only to regrets, then what might have been fun turns into emptiness.

Goals Can Make the Difference

If you do not know where you are going, you are liable to end up someplace you do not want to be. Many people believe they cannot help what they do, or what they are, or what they turn out to be. "After all," they say, "according to the psychology books, I am the product of heredity and environment, a helpless cork upon the giant sea."

Do not suppose that psychology suggests helplessness. Quite the opposite! The concepts offered by psychology are tools with which to act. We are not mere products of heredity and environment. We are free-thinking selves, capable of managing our own behavior and influencing the behavior of others. We have a very obvious say in what we become.

It is true that life may be at times a giant and stormy sea, and there are people who let themselves be little more than helpless corks. But there are others who work at being ships with compasses and sturdy rudders. Those who lack realistic goals drift aimlessly in life. Others know where they want to go and stay headed in the right direction. Where do you want to go? What do you want in life? What do you value most? What are your goals? Security? Perhaps an opportunity to help others and make the world better? Or just to grow up and enjoy the freedom of being an adult? These are common answers.

There are the teens who say, "I want to have a little fun before I get married and have to settle down." I sincerely hope all who say such things do not feel marriage must be the end of fun. Happiness should come not only with the short-term goals of here and now. It should certainly come after marriage. And it also should come with goals we will not dream up for another ten or fifty years.

But some people think of happiness in a very limited way, in terms of kicks and moments of emotional release. This is a major problem for a great number of teens. They get so involved in the urges of the moment that they neglect the goals necessary for repeated fun and still-to-be-discovered happiness.

There is nothing wrong with having kicks—kicks that really work for us, kicks that do not backfire and cause us more trouble than good. We all need moments of emotional release, chances to unwind and let off steam. But we need to discover fun that does not have regrettable consequences which interfere with future happiness. We need to discover fun that not only makes us feel better at the time but also helps insure future happiness.

The idea of lasting happiness can be approached from many different points of view. Most briefly stated, it is a life-long extension of the seven ingredients for a good time noted in Chapter Two. It is especially dependent on the seventh ingredient, *the look ahead.* For happiness is very much concerned with having an intelligent set of goals, in going where you want to go, and in becoming the somebody you want to be.

Security—What Is It?

You will find adults quick to tell you, "Kids don't know the value of money these days." And there is truth here, of a sort. The teens of today escaped the depression years, and few of them know what it is to be down-and-out, wondering whether the soup should be watered so there will be enough to go around.

Yet, there is just as much truth to the statement, "Kids don't know the worthlessness of money these days." We should learn to use our money wisely and gain experience in what it takes to earn it. But at the same time, we should understand its limitations.

If we believe it to be so, money does buy security—a limited temporary security. Exactly how much money it takes to buy security varies with different individuals and families. It depends on personal values and on desired standards of living. While one person feels well off as long as the bills are paid, another may feel destitute without two late-model cars and a few thousand dollars in the bank.

In selecting your goals, you will want to take into consideration your future financial security. However, do not let it dominate your thinking. Be aware of pitfalls. Financial security is not security in all things. It does not guarantee answers to the needs higher up the scale of the hierarchy of needs. It does not guarantee a loving family, satisfaction in your work, or peace of mind. It does not even guarantee that it will last.

The guideposts leading to security are never certain or absolutely clear. A change in world conditions or technology can topple the best of castles. You must expect to be mislead from time to time. Then you must be ready to make changes in your plans and in your goals.

Unfortunately, when some people speak of security they mean comfort. And comfort is not famous for resulting in security. It has been known to put people to sleep in the midst of insecure situations.

At the opposite extreme from comfort there is what Booker T. Washington once called "the advantage of disadvantages." There is also "the security of insecurities." Handicaps and insecurities have provided motivations leading to full, productive, and relatively secure lives.

To sense a lack of complete security is an indication of intelligence and mental health. Or put another way, to feel totally secure in all things is a sign of ignorance or extreme defensive behavior. And failure to recognize real threat and danger can make us, in fact, less secure.

To Be of Help to Others

Some of the saddest tales I know are of sparkling, enthusiastic young people who sincerely set out to help people in need, only to become cynical, beaten down, and disillusioned before they were midway in their lives. What went wrong?

The basic idea was sound enough: to want to help people, to try to make this a better world. We cannot intelligently want for ourselves without wanting for other people. There is too great an interrelation of people and peoples in this modern world.

It takes more than a desire to help, however. Some people were worn down by impossible tasks. They encountered lethargy and lack of interest in those they had to depend on for support. They fell victim to a world in conflict. They were defeated by external factors over which they had no control. It is likely that others defeated themselves. They plunged in to try to help, but they had not given enough thought to what, why, and how.

To be of help takes an understanding of what help means. Real help is the answering of needs. Understanding this requires an understanding of the hierarchy of needs. Real help is answering the urgent needs of the present, while building provisions for answering the higher, unseen needs of the future. Commonly, people with good intentions try to help by imposing their own elevated morality on others whose needs are at a much more basic level than a need for self-respect or even a need for love. This is not to say that these others will never have a need for morality. But people who want to help must focus on the needs and feelings of those to be helped. They must have the wisdom and the training to know how to do the work at hand.

To be of help and to keep at it for any length of time requires a grasp of the limitations of both the helper and the helped. Sometimes we expect too much. When I am carried away with anger because I cannot do the impossible a psychologist friend tells me, "Don, we can't save the whole world, and we're lucky if we can save ourselves." The helplessness which must be endured at times when you truly want to help is not easy to bear.

Offsetting the limitations of people, however, are their tremendous potentials—what they can do and what they can become. People can be helped. By removing the threats to their basic survival they can be brought to sense needs higher up the scale. They can be brought to think more intelligently. Rather than gather fury, because others do not do right by them, they can be helped to help themselves and to share responsibility for others.

Surely, there are obstacles to helping. There is lack of support and lack of understanding. There is lack of knowledge of how best to help. There are human limitations. But people who want to be of genuine and continuing help must realize that this is the way it is. This is not a reason to be discouraged. It is additional reason to keep at it. We work both in spite of and because of some obstacles.

The Freedom of Being an Adult

"I'll be glad when I'm finally old enough not to have people talking down to me and telling me what to do all the time." "Man, I'll be glad in a couple of years when I can afford a car of my own." "If we were only old enough to get married!" In one way or another, most teens look forward to the time when they will be recognized as adult.

Physical maturity and legal age come with the passage of time—whether we want them or not. What is sadly overlooked, however, is that they can come without any increase of freedom from having to be told what to do, without being able to afford a car, and without much hope of having a happy marriage. Physical maturity and legal age are not guarantees of added freedom to do or get what we want.

Actually, what might at first glance seem to be a look to happier times in the future is little more than the defense mechanism of fantasy for some people. Some rationalize and daydream that things will be better after they get away from home, after they get out of school, or after they are old enough to get a job. They fantasize that things will be better but do nothing to prepare for it and make it so.

They talk big about wanting more freedom. But they really do not mean it. Whenever they find they have freedom, they try to get rid of it. They are unable to cope with the responsibilities that go with freedom. They try to find a leader, a crowd, or a phony cause to follow—someone or some group to take on the responsibilities and tell them what to do.

They seem threatened by facts or ideas that might help them make their own decisions. They fear the burden of thinking things through. They want someone to take care of them. Someone who will let them do what they want to do, *up to a point,* but who will keep them from being hurt. Someone who will shelter them from being hurt. Someone who will shelter them as a mother and protect them as a father, and make it unnecessary for them to grow up. Someone to blame when things go wrong.

Look around and you will see people so limited in their development and in comprehension of their selves that they do not understand what freedom is. They see it as a sort of special, private right to do as they please, regardless of who is hurt, regardless of how much they steal freedom from those around them. They think it is a right to take without giving, to be paid without earning.

Freedom is not the good and easy life. It does not mean automatic liberation from want and from frustration. For some it turns out to mean the opposite. Freedom offers opportunity, and not everyone takes advantage of opportunity.

Freedom is a privilege of choice. It is having a part in determining what we will do and what we will become. It is the opportunity to work toward our own goals. It is having a part in determining what the groups to which we belong will do and what our families, our communities, our country, and our world will become.

Freedom in its truest sense is something we must use wisely today if we wish increased freedom and a better life tomorrow. We must have goals for what we want ourselves and our world to be. We must take advantage of the opportunities to work toward these goals.

How High Is Your Personal Star?

Teens are forever being advised to "shoot for the stars." "Set your sights high," they are told. "Set your goals higher than you think you can reach, and even if you fall short of your mark, you will still be farther than you would have been otherwise. Plan to be president; you might make mayor. Plan to marry the prettiest woman (or the most handsome man); you might get her sister (or his brother)."

I cannot buy such an approach. It leads to failure and disappointment. It puts satisfaction and happiness out of reach. I know too many people who have good, full lives by most standards, but who are bitterly unhappy because they are not as prominent, powerful, or wealthy as they thought they had to be. Such an approach also tends to make you introject the values of the adviser and accept his standards as to what is high, rather than deciding what is high and best for yourself.

I say repeatedly, "Don't sell yourself short." You may have much more on the ball than you or anyone else supposes. Be optimistic. Shoot for the presidency, the prettiest woman (or man), or the decathlon, if this is what you want. But do not get so carried away that you jump off a cliff, firm in the belief that if you "set your mind to it" and flap your arms fast enough you will fly.

Base your goals on intelligence. If you think intelligently about your goals, you will set them high in terms of what you value, in terms of what counts most in your life. And this is as it should be. As a science teacher once responded when discussing such things, "Stars are useful in determining direction. But they aren't very good as goals—unless you have a spacecraft."

Goals Change

Once a mother called me and said, a trifle harshly, "Don't tell my daughter she shouldn't be a doctor. She made her mind up to be a doctor when she was five years old, and she's going to be a doctor. You don't know the drive that girl has. She's not going to change to something else, no matter what."

I had not told the girl she should not be a doctor. I had suggested that she gain awareness of the obstacles in her path, of the investment in training ahead, and of what it means, day after day, to be a physician. I had suggested that she keep an open mind to other occupations she might prefer. And I suggested that she bring up her grades and develop an adequate plan for becoming a physician, if this goal was what she really wanted.

I have an aversion to 5-year-old minds dominating the lives of teenagers and adults. The fact that a person made up his or her mind a long time ago to do something is poor evidence for deciding it is still the best thing to do. Decisions are most likely to be best when we utilize the very latest additions and improvements in our mental machinery. We get smarter every day.

As we grow and as our world changes, our needs and values change. These are linked closely to our goals. One changes with the other. What we need and value we try to attain and keep. What we do not need and value we try to avoid or get rid of.

Reevaluate from time to time. In the light of new-found needs and values, consider your successes and failures along the way. Give yourself time to think. Do not make impulsive changes. But when it is the logical thing to do, act. If you understand the concept of the hierarchy of needs, you know that goals should not be fixed and unchanging. A logical change should never be considered a failure or defeat. Remember, when you make a change, move *toward* something, not only away from something. Put the emphasis where it belongs—on the new and better goal.

Our Fun-Oriented Society

Good and serious-minded people insist that this is a work-oriented society, that everything points to and gains meaning through work. And I hesitate to quarrel with people who want to think along those lines. I did a poster once that read, "Work is love that can be seen."

But without denying the worth of work, this book is here to tell you, at this time and in this country, that ours is a fun-oriented society. The emphasis as I view it is on good times, satisfactions, and fun. Work, it turns out, is just one of the indispensable activities that helps achieve the fun we seek.

Now, whether work becomes a fun thing in itself depends, I suggest, on how much of it matches up with the elements of the fun formula. Some jobs have all the ingredients; some have little more than a paycheck that makes it possible for the employee to make use of the other half of the waking hours and add the missing ingredients needed to round things out.

In any event, planning and preparation for work is going to have a lot to do with having fun. The free-ride kids of all ages always luck out when it comes to the look ahead.

With all of the fabulous new books on careers and career education available, we will not dwell on such subjects here. But any promising *look ahead to more fun* in the future always includes a *look ahead to work*. The soundness of fun orientations rests heavily on decisions and preparations for careers.

School Guidance Counselors

You should expect help from your school counselors in developing realistic goals, especially in the educational and career areas. They have access to your school records and the results of the various standardized tests you have taken through the years. They should be able to provide you with helpful facts and ideas and, most important, give you an opportunity to discuss your concerns frankly in a confidential setting. But do not be disappointed if counselors do not give you all the answers. Counselors serve you best when they help you to make decisions rather than when they make them for you.

Tests and records are useful tools, but they are only tools. After discussing them with you, counselors should be able to give you some ideas to think about. They should be able to tell you something of the odds for or against you in different fields. They may point out unseen weaknesses or strong points that you should take into consideration. They may help you see yourself and your world a bit more clearly. But they cannot tell you what you should be or do. Your look ahead, when it comes to a choice of a career, must come from you.

Chapter Fourteen

THE PREJUDICE THING

"Look out for them purples, whites, pinks, blacks, yellows, reds, tans, or whatever color you don't happen to be. Then there are those people with the different hair. And the ones with the unfamiliar way of speaking. And those from that other neighborhood. And even those people of the opposite sex. You are better than they are, and all those things that are said about them have to be the way it is, you know?

Or do you?"

We hang a lot of stuff on one another that is not deserved. Then in righteous defense, the victims strike back and become the attackers. All sides get hurt. All rationalize with greater unfairness.

Over and over, we are hindered from being somebody of recognized stature and worth because of the forces related to prejudice. Some of us even stop trying in any constructive way and turn to excusing our own failings by blaming others. Some of us feel persecution, both real and imagined, so keenly that we will not let ourselves experience the freedom and fun that is available.

When fun is always kept just out of reach, hate is an easy thing to come by. And prejudice of the worst kind explodes in every direction, generating as in the frustration-aggression cycle.

What Is Prejudice?

Prejudice is usually thought to mean unfair, damaging opinions and attitudes toward another person or group. But it is an inadequate term that never seems to help much of anything. Used with a mixture of half-truths and distortions, it prompts more of the same. It often confuses and keeps us from getting at realities and eventual solutions.

If you look at the word, "pre-judice," it obviously means *prejudgment* or judgment beforehand; that is, to judge something in advance. It means to judge people or situations before there is sufficient information to be completely accurate and fair. Imperfect as this practice may be, it is routine, functional, and necessary in life. It is experienced as being safer than going into each new situation with a completely open mind, as though we had learned nothing whatsoever in the past that might apply to the new situation.

Tonight, suppose you are standing on your front steps and a giant of a man comes running toward you with a long knife in his hand, laughing hysterically. If you are much like me, you are probably going to step back in the house, lock the door, and call the police. Now you might find out later that the man was a great inventor who had just discovered how to make a butcher knife that never gets dull. He may have just wanted to share his new invention with you. And it may have been terribly unfair and downright prejudiced of you to shut him out and call the police when he was just trying to be nice and friendly. But no one can dare or find time to risk postponing every judgment until all the facts are in.

Better Words Make Better Sense

At best, the term "prejudice" is too generalized. If we mean to say that someone is treating another unfairly, then we ought to specify how and why, not merely generalize at the level of name-calling.

Perhaps the dynamics involved in prejudice can be viewed more precisely as self-defense mechanisms. For example, to say that Nazis were prejudiced against the Jews in Germany in the 1930's provides a very limited picture. It suggests little or nothing of causes and reasons. We come closer to understanding when the term *"scapegoating"* is used and when it is recognized that the Jews suffered displaced aggression resulting from the frustrations of the time. Fantastic rationalizations were developed to support super-race concepts and label the Jews inferior. The intolerable guilt felt by Nazi leaders was projected on the innocent. People dissociated, holding one set of standards for themselves and a conflicting set for their neighbors. Germans identified with their leaders and introjected the goals and rationalizations of the Nazi Party. In this setting, former nobodies became fantasied somebodies called storm troopers. Through force they imposed their highly rationalized superiority over people who had earned esteem as creative, productive men and women.

It may be appropriate at this time to mention the late Sigmund Freud at this time—the father of psychoanalysis who is credited with originating many of the most basic concepts in this book. Dr. Freud was a minority group member. He felt sharp injustice and discrimination throughout his life, both because he was a Jew and because he was a brilliant, courageous thinker. His great strides toward truth in his day were feared by most authorities as assaults on the accepted professional notions of the day. He asserted the life-long normalcy of sex and theorized how faulty attitudes and intense guilt feelings in this area can result in mental illness. Because of the progress he initiated, he became famous throughout the world. But in Germany his books were burned. And when the Nazi armies invaded Austria, his own historic professional library was destroyed and his birthplace burned; he was held for ransom, and his sisters were murdered. Again prejudice seems a totally inadequate word.

Race. Who Wins?

"Who discovered America?" Now there is another stupid question that says where we are in the prejudice thing.

If Columbus or Leif Ericson is the answer sought, the question should be, "Who was the first European to visit the continent now called America?" It would make as much sense to ask, "Who discovered Europe?" when intending to ask, "Who was the first American Indian to visit Europe?"

Such single-point-of-view misrepresentations are infuriating when imposed on people they slight and neglect. Imagine having someone infer that your people were nothing until some other people found them. Perhaps you are one who does not have to imagine. Textbooks, laws, and general understanding should not ignore the existence of people. All races and cultures are of significance in the evolution of greatness. Blind assertions that only some of us can really be worthwhile are destructive and hurt all of us in the long run. In order to be, we must let others be. To be somebody important, we have to let others find importance. Cut someone else down, and we do not raise ourselves but only live in a lesser world. We have to let importance be shared—with all but those who try to make it by fanning old arsons.

"Sure, I'm mean," I heard a boy tell a social worker who was trying to help him. "But I'm so full of hate because of all the bad things all those other people did to my people in the past."

"Garbage!" she found herself replying. "Don't ask me to fall for that dumb bit about obligations to feel guilty for the sins of our fathers. My father deserted my mother and me when I was so young I don't even remember him. If he did something wrong, or his father, or his, or his, go see them. Don't lay it on me."

"Well, it isn't all in the past," he countered. "I have reason to get back at the people of your race."

"Reason?" she asked. "You think you can hurt someone and then excuse it all simply because he is the same color as someone who hurt you? Not likely. What do you do when someone of your own color hurts you? Hit yourself?"

"No."

"So where's the sense to it?"

Revenge for so-called prejudice—past or present—never excuses crime. And using revenge as an excuse only divides people further and fosters the same sort of vengeful hate in more and more people. The feuds of past generations are stupid crosses for present generations. It is a terrible commentary on our times that some who have great potential for pulling it together for a happier future have simply slipped to the consuming sickness of carrying forward the hatreds of the past.

There is, of course, some things we should bring forward. Any sane approach demands that we retain the happy, productive foundations of our heritage. So save the good and throw out the garbage. All races and cultures have greatness in their pasts—moments of pride and people of wisdom and accomplishment. Books and schools must do more to help us discover and share the wide heritage of the human race. And through it all, perhaps we can see the needs that make us similar rather than dwell on the phoniness that seems to make us different.

Striving toward this wider view of things may seem an idealism that can never be attained. But it is surely more productive than the miserable game of introjecting what some proclaimed leader declares is the superior us. Dissipating creative energies in revenge and revolt can put us right back with our arms in the air, playing superrace, surrendering actual freedom for the raving promises of some führer.

Being Somebody As a Member of Your Sex

Remember back in seventh grade all the trouble some boys had trying to be somebody around girls who were bigger, stronger, and seemingly smarter than they were? At that age, of course, girls have an undeniable edge on boys; they pass through puberty and physically mature a year or two younger than boys.

In a variety of ways throughout life, a person's sex has to do with being somebody. *Whether* a person is male or female and *how* that person is male or female are fundamental in the development of significant identity. How a person appears as a member of one sex or the other and how he or she acts and feels about it are vital in defining a person's worth. Sexual feelings, attitudes, beliefs, and self-concepts, true or false, learned or unlearned, discussed openly or kept secret forever, are entwined contributors to the fragile persons we want to be.

A Jesuit priest, once talking about such things with a respected colleague, told of a boy he found skipping gym. It came out that the boy felt a shameful self-consciousness about not being as developed as the other boys and, also, being different in appearance because he was not circumcised.

"Look around you," the priest told him. "Look at all the faces. Everyone is different. The shapes of the noses and the chins are different. And the shapes of the bodies are different. God made us all different. And the same is true of sex organs. All are different. All mature at somewhat different ages. So perhaps, we feel a little uncomfortable about it, especially when we don't understand. But no one should feel ashamed. Different is not bad. It's just different."

And any girl who has experienced gang showers or who has had to make decisions about padded bras knows that girls have similar feelings about being different. Being markedly different from others of the same sex can prompt us to feel superior or inferior—a confident somebody or a doomed nobody. But it isn't so much the bodily difference that causes the feelings. It is the attitudes or prejudgments we hold in regard to these differences in ourselves and others that determine the nature and the extent of such feelings. This is true of feelings related to differences *within* the one half of the world that is our own sex. And it also is true related to the differences *between* one sex and the other.

Our attitudes and prejudgments about how our sex differs from the opposite sex have a great deal to do with our feelings about ourselves and our own relative importance. Through second-hand information and through direct experience, contrasting attitudes and prejudgments take shape in all of us, though differently in different people in different settings.

Some of us see a close bond with the opposite sex as an indispensable part of becoming worthy, but others find importance by denying any need for such bonds and by asserting superiority over the other half. Some devote themselves to being one with the opposite sex. Some shout loudly that to be somebody of worth they must be liberated from obligations and ties with them.

Angry rejections are commonplace. Most of us have had moments of disappointment and frustration in our relationships. Voiced prejudice soon follows.

"Girls! Never trust a girl. Build you up and make you feel like you are the greatest. Then there they are, taking up with some other dudes. And you always are supposed to treat them with respect. Girls tell you they want things equal, but they still expect you to do things for them that you wouldn't do for a boy. The boys get stuck with paying for a date while the girls have most of the say on what to do. They open you up, then treat you like dirt." We've all heard something of this sort.

And we have often heard: "Boys! Never trust a boy. One day saying everything is beautiful and sacred between you, and the next, blabbing it around to other boys like a filthy joke. And they get so much more freedom than a girl does even when they can't handle it. Bluff and big talk is all they are. Bunch of immature babies is what they are, and the girls aren't supposed to lay that on them, not if we want to get along. And when it comes to dating, we have to wait around and hope we are asked. We're supposed to play at being helpless, but that doesn't make anyone count for anything."

At first glance it may seem incomprehensible that people who have great need for each other by their very nature would be able to feel hate and prejudice toward the objects of this need. But where there is need—especially deep, urgent, basic need—there is potential for intense frustration, fierce aggression, and frantic self-defense mechanisms.

Person's Lib

Time magazine once provided a quote from a feminist that hints at a common attitude: "In almost any woman you can unearth an incredible fury. And it's an anger that can be a powerful radicalizing force."

I have every confidence that this is true, and further, that the word "man" can be substituted for the word "woman." There is in almost every *person* a potentially furious response to injustice, a potential toward the frustration-aggression cycle, and a potential life-or-death defense action against attack.

Currently complicating the relationship between the sexes, a transition is now under way in which women and men are finding new freedom from the age-old roles. No longer is it demanded that the man be the so-called head of the family, the provider. No longer is it demanded that the woman tend the fires and maintain the home. It becomes more and more acceptable for the caring of the children, food preparation, household chores, and general support of the family to be shared by both husband and wife. And it becomes more and more possible for both women and men to have full-time salaried careers in any field their individual capabilities permit, regardless of traditional definitions of masculinity or femininity. The day of male telephone operators and female mechanics has arrived. Many industries search for new employees who are willing to cross the traditional career lines.

In the midst of such dramatic attempts at change in society, confusion and conflict of values are certain to result on every front. Many people are frightened at being pulled into new circumstances they do not want. Many are furious because of remaining obstacles they consider to be unfair. Some fear an awful loss of central beauty in their lives and are severely depressed by attempts at philosophical destruction of what they see as close, meaningful, sensitive relationships between the sexes. Some band together into power groups to support and defend their views, sometimes under such procedural titles as *consciousness-raising*. Action may at first be intended to develop awareness of facts and to organize for intelligent action. But when groups dwell on injustice and bitterness, painful repressions are dredged up in the distorted form of emotionally expressed rationalizations which scapegoat the opposite sex.

Common bonds of generalized hate develop, sometimes stemming from injustices suffered because of actions of the opposite sex and sometimes stemming from self-hatred that is repressed and projected onto others.

Motivations are complex. What people do may seem to contradict true facts and underlying causes. *Reaction formations* are common. Deeply unhappy people, feeling rejected from what they unconsciously want most to do and to be, superficially cling to importance by rationalizing ugliness and undesirability into what they unconsciously desire.

When people feel trapped, bored, or threatened by their situation, they naturally look around to find someone or something to blame. But this makes sense only insofar as it suggests intelligent emphasis in working to make things better. If there is something to blame, something at fault, something or someone who is really the cause of the trouble, then it may be a logical step to figure that out as a part of the process of making things better. But blaming does not do much to help, not by itself. And often it makes things worse. Between the sexes, blaming, especially when it is not totally justified, drives people farther apart. And for most people, additional alienation serves no purpose and answers no healthy need.

Men and women now are able to express an honest sexuality more than ever before. Shame rooted in ignorance need not plague people as in the past. Pretense at inferiority, subservience, or helplessness is no longer prescribed as a part of the female role. Men are no longer required to be insensitive, authoritarian, and domineering to prove masculinity. The way is open for sexes to discover a unity of genuineness together. To lose it all through hate and prejudice would be the ultimate tragedy. As we strive to alter laws and customs to make possible the personal fulfillment of people—through the best of what "women's lib," "men's lib," or whatever—the dangers of prejudice are always with us.

Be Real—and Realistic

"Yeah, I know," said the black man next to me. "You are one of those guys who thinks he loves everybody." It was at a conference in San Francisco, and up to that point we had not accomplished much. There were seven of us at the table, including a grey-haired lady from Taiwan, a white principal from Wisconsin whose son-in-law was black, and four black students from San Francisco State College.

The man who spoke had shot down every suggestion I had made so far in the discussion. I was feeling normal reactions to the frustration that he was causing me.

"No," I responded. "I do not love everybody. And I haven't made my mind up whether or not I like you. But I sure as hell do not automatically hate you because of color. And I think that's what you are putting on me. If I don't like you, you made it on your own. OK?"

He squinted, studied my eyes, shrugged, and said, "Fair enough." And things started to move forward.

This example shows that attempting to define what is going on can sometimes help make things better. You cannot proceed on phoniness. In this situation my initial attempts at getting along and trying to keep my cool came off as phoniness. In my response I recognized the existence of prejudice. Defensively, and probably incorrectly, I had put it on him, and I had blundered out the message that I was not perfect but I was trying and wanted him to try, too. Happily, it was an acceptable communication, and we began working together.

An acceptance of the existence and normalcy of prejudice can often be the beginning of making things better—if the acceptance is realistic. Prejudice exists and will continue to exist. Some people your age are going to be prejudiced against some people my age. Some people who worship God differently, and some who do not believe in His existence, are going to be prejudiced against one another. People who have different sexual feelings and inclinations, people who look different from one another, people who love athletic sports and people who do not are going to be inclined to hold unjust prejudgments about one another. This is nothing new.

Historically, a lot of people came to this country attempting to escape prejudice. By modern standards, they were very prejudiced people themselves. And if you know anything about the past relationships of Indian tribes, you know there was a lot of prejudice among the people who were already here before Caucasians, Orientals, blacks, and others began to arrive.

Perhaps the phoniest part of prejudice is the inference that only "they," the bad guys, the people on the other side, are to blame. This common short-circuit thinking leads us to the faulty conclusion that if we could somehow be rid of them, all those people who do not look and think like us, then things would be all right. But the fact is, nobody looks or thinks exactly as we do. Criticizing those who are different offers no solutions. It is endless, often pointless, and self-consuming. The revolutionists, who merely attempt to shift persecution from one group to another, attain at most a temporary vengeance which will turn to cut them down as well.

Near the close of the San Francisco conference, the grey-haired Chinese teacher commented to the young people at our table: "I have traveled all around the world. In no place do you have as much freedom and opportunity as in this country, your America. But it is saddening to me," she said, "that you do not seem to enjoy it. Instead, you ignore it. You seem to need to not see that it is there. You use it, you use this exceptional freedom, to protest that you do not have it."

The Major Question

Is it really necessary to feel superior in order to be somebody? If we are going to cope with prejudice, this is a question we will have to work out, individually and socially, within the groups to which we belong.

The hope and goal is that we can be of significance to ourselves and to each other without having to lord it over other people. I suggest that this significance must be on the basis of our productivity, our contribution to the world, and the help we can be to the people around us. Genuine somebodies have no need for prejudice. They strive to relate to others and to work with them, not to alienate them or declare them enemies.

There are massive problems to be solved which require the joint effort of all—overpopulation, food and energy shortages, pollution, and the frustrations and aggressions of other countries having even more explosive problems than we have. The hate-revenge drive of the jungle can put us right back in the jungle, a new mod jungle where nothing can grow. As expressed by Martin Luther King, "We must live together as brothers or perish together as fools."

Chapter Fifteen

DRUG SCENE GRAFFITI

"We're getting a lot of young kids now," a former addict in her mid-20s told me. She was then heading up a successful rehabilitation program in New England. "It's, well, pretty scary. And I have a lot of theories why. Seeing what I see and knowing what happened with me, I think a lot of it is because of the repression of emotions. The kids have never really been shown that to express themselves emotionally and share how they feel is a, well, its an education, really. They should learn how to deal with feelings. They should talk about how they feel about themselves at an early age. They should learn how to deal with the decisions they're going to have to make, and learn how to cope with a lot of things around them. I never learned, you know."

Because drug use is about trying to feel better, about trying to have fun, about trying to put down the pain, about trying to understand yourself and the people around you in greater depth, about trying to face up to mistakes and about trying to find ways to go on to better things, this book is very much about drug-related problems.

"If you want to hear about drugs," said the former addict in New England, as she talked with teenagers, "go down to the police station. They have those little suitcases that they open up and show you what the drugs are like. But if you want to talk about why you act the way you do and why you feel the need to get high and get away from yourself, that's what I want to talk about."

The most significant questions on the human scene do not deal with either the effects of the various drugs—enlightening or demolishing—or with last night's price for a balloon on Haight Street. Instead, the basic, relevant questions for the individual are, "Must I, will I, come to depend on drugs and drug-oriented activities for my highs, for my fun in life? Or can I develop productive, caring relationships and work out life-styles based on genuine, contributing experiences in the world of reality?"

Drug Use—Why?

"You've got to have something to turn to," a student told me recently. "Like if your parents are fighting and yelling at you, or if you are completely bored and can't cut it in school. Or like with my friend who wants to do right by the girl, and there's no way. No way. So you got to have somewhere to turn." He thought in silence for a time. Then, "For some kids though, it's more that they feel they just have to do something, to have some excitement. They just feel so down that they've got to find something. And the stuff is there. I mean, at home, always wine and liquor, and pills around like you wouldn't believe. And out there," he gestured, "you can usually buy anything you want."

People always see causes in terms of their own needs, experiences, observations, and individual circumstances. But situations differ. And causes vary with the complexities of individual personalities and the interacting setting.

Inner psychological problems are probably always there as causes, but by their very nature, repressed and not understood, they are seldom expressed with any logic or order that might lead to solutions. Many people feel that it is better to run away from such complexities, to find people and social situations to blame, and to use defensive mechanisms rather than face up to problems. Many people tend to evade or fantasize rather than to persist at attempting to find satisfaction through reality. The impulse to escape is often cited as a reason for drug use.

Escape from what? Pain? Boredom? Authority? From parents "who don't care" or "care too much"? Pressures to achieve? From problems adults seem unable or ashamed and afraid to deal with?

Escape from sex? From love? Prejudice? Financial problems? Depression and general lack of fun?

Escape from any and all of these is a fair answer. When we are frustrated, our basic impulse is to fight or to escape. And drugs are often an escape response to frustration.

In our unprecedented world of unappreciated luxury, drugs also have come to be promises of fun. And the two motivations—escape and quest for fun—have become mingled. As advertisements in the magazines suggest to us, whether or not we can afford the trip, "ESCAPE TO FUN."

Elsewhere along the scale of the human situation, drugs are not seen as a means of escape but more as a hope for more intense fulfillment and a reaching out for higher thrills in the midst of already having fun. Clearly, as people on the scene have told me and as evidenced in many surveys, fun is the central reason for using drugs. And I submit that it may be the central reason for not using drugs, as well.

But what is fun, when it comes to drugs? Perhaps the seven points of the fun formula can help to clarify.

Action

"At the time, to begin with, it wasn't that I had big problems. Now, yes. Then, no. But that day, it was more that I didn't have much of anything to do. I was just bored, in a dumb, childish way, maybe, now looking back on it. There must have been other things I could've done, something else to do. Anyway, then, I was looking for I don't know what. Something to do. And then getting into something I guess I wanted and knew I didn't want. If that makes any sense?"

Similar words have come from people telling of a first injection of heroin in a ghetto alley and from people telling of lonely experiments with medicine-chest pills on rainy afternoons in plush homes in the suburbs. Boredom and the basic need for activity are contributing forces in a wide variety of settings.

Action quite naturally tops the list as an obvious component of fun. But the grand, marvelous world of our present provides us with fabulous artificial substitutes for real, firsthand experience. Miracles are within reach in every direction, and we have learned to take all of them completely for granted. Our capacity to travel in our imagination, to experience vicariously, and to think dreams within the mind are miracles of a sort. And miracles, indeed, are those wonderful tools, devices, and enterprises that guide us in our inner actions—the television, the radio, the movies, the record player, and the very book in your hands.

Now, add to all of this the fact that most young people have had it relatively easy. They have not had to put in as much as they have taken out. Most have had adequate food, clothing, and shelter without being required to work to earn it. Most have lived in relative security within America without the necessity of serving in the armed forces. Our good but relatively unappreciated life has taught some of us, at least, that there is an easy road, a magical solution for everything. And out of our science-fiction fantasies has come the supposed magic of sensational activity through drugs.

Drugs, then, have become part of the something to do for a substantial number of the young. "And once you've been using," I was told by one who knew, "but say you are cured, time is always heavy on you. You have a day when there's nothing to do, or you're lonely and there's no one there, and you have to have something. And it's not only drugs you get thinking about, not just the feeling you have after you take drugs. It's all the routine, all the things that go into it. It's finding something to rip off to get the money, making the rounds to find the supply. There's lots to do to just get there."

Once sampled, the drive to be doing something is often compulsively directed toward drug-oriented activity. Having nothing to do offers intolerable temptation, even when firm decisions have been made to avoid further use. In order to stay away from drugs, before or after addictive use—whether physical or psychological addiction— it is imperative to stay busy, to be occupied with other things.

Discovery

"I'm really getting hassled by a few kids around here because I won't use drugs," a girl told me in conversation at a midnight rock session at the most recent White House Conference on Youth.

"Here I am on the Drug Task Force and I haven't even tried any of the stuff we are talking about, they say. And they were getting to me, until one of the boys whom I especially respect said, 'She hasn't tried dying yet, either. There's another in-depth experience.' "

Different drugs do different things. Some excite, some depress, and some cause hallucinations. Specific drugs may affect different people in quite different ways. A common example most people are familiar with is the effect of alcohol on different individuals. In one dimension, drunks range from generous lovers to angry warriors.

Drugs that put aside conscious controls and delve into the repressions of the unconscious do provide potential for discovery. And some people are into drugs for this reason, so they say. But listening to some of them, I get images of explorers attacking priceless fossil beds with pickaxes and children pulling apart an atomic pile just to see what is inside.

LSD induces an escape state much like schizophrenia—a serious mental illness during which the individual may see and hear things that do not exist in external reality. When such a trip is taken with a psychiatrist at hand, it can be argued to have possible discovery benefits, in spite of various risks. When taken in unpredictable sugar-cube quantity and quality, and without psychiatric supervision and follow-up, it is hazardous, and the supposed self-discoveries are so weighted with autistic restructuring that they are liable to be more destructive than beneficial. Commonly documented consequences include terror states, uncontrolled violence, murder, suicide, extensive hospitalization, and severe personality disturbances. Yet there are people who relate what they believe to be fulfilling self-discovery.

"We don't go for that mind-expanding stuff," I remember being told by former heroin addicts in San Francisco. "We see different things. Like, they tell you about all those beautiful colors and flowers and love-everybody feelings. But we see our daddy kicking our mother in the stomach . . . toilets that don't work . . . rats on the bed . . . different things."

"We know what each of the drugs will do," one sophisticated boy in quite another group insisted. "We know all about them. When someone uses a drug, he knows what he is doing and what will happen."

"Off the street?" a girl in the group challenged. "Come on. Seven buys of mescaline last week. Peyote was supposed to be the big thing. Different kids made buys in different places. And nobody had mescaline. They checked it out. They have this service where you can take drugs and have them tell you what it is," she clarified for me. "And there was a wild bunch of stuff. But nobody had mescaline. They didn't know what they were taking."

Street drugs often provide a little something extra or sometimes offer surprises. Freud, for example, before he arrived at his theory of psychoanalysis, researched and personally experienced a new wonder drug called cocaine. Initial findings caused him to recommend it to his friends and his family, which in later years (using his words), led him to "grave reproaches." Discoveries in the drug world can lead to regret.

It is sometimes autistically overlooked that drug use can hinder and prevent normal development and learning. Kenneth Graham of the San Mateo Schools, suggests, for example, the importance of what he terms a "calloused psyche." Unhappy things happen to all of us, he points out. But "as time goes by you find you are still alive, that the world is not as bad as it was, that you haven't been rejected by everyone because your girl friend dumped you. And then it happens again, some other time, someplace else. But this time it's not as traumatic because you've got a callous over that bruised spot and you've learned to handle things. And as time goes on you learn to handle a lot of things . . . you would not have been able to handle if you didn't have these callouses. And part of the problem in taking drugs and escaping from all this, they never get the callouses. Each time it's a raw wound with the new experience because they retreat from the situation."

Emotional Experiences

If there is one flaw above all others in our cultural structure, one thing that will cause people to use and abuse drugs more than any other, it is the lack of built-in provision for adequate, need-fulfilling emotional experiences as a regular part of every individual's life. Expression of emotionality in many instances is blocked, expressly forbidden, and labeled taboo. And there is a shortage of outlets that are both socially accepted and rewarding.

The glory of athletics, for example, is not for everyone. And even though physical educators might declare that everyone has a chance to participate, I hardly think that anyone would make the investment that is now expended on those who show talent and interest in sports on those that do not.

Sexual activity is an area of confusion. The general population is left so constantly unfulfilled that advertisers need only to allude to sex in order to have instant attention. And many people are so destructively oriented that they find it impossible to express themselves sexually without using drugs—to "loosen up" or to blame it on.

Churches and religions do not reach everyone, and some of those that do actually restrict and suppress emotional expression much more than encourage it. Technology confines work to less energetic tasks and minimizes physical exertion of the sort for which emotions prepare us. Crowded, overpopulated conditions further restrict us and demand that we stay cool and passive in our daily lives.

For a substantial number of people, drug use has arrived as a seemingly acceptable substitute for emotional expression. Although the words of established authority say, "No," parental and peer models too often say, "Everybody's doing it." And the media continually link drug use with excitement and fun.

To some, at particular moments in their lives, the risks and consequences of drug use seem minimal compared with the risks and consequences of attempting to work out life-styles of adequate emotional expression any other way. Drug use requires no ball diamonds, mountains, or battlefields. It requires no member of the opposite sex, who may shame you if you go too far or not far enough, or who may break your heart and leave you for another. Drugs just bring illusions of ecstacy, without the awesome risks of entering into the real game of life. It is tragic when chemically stimulated substitutes are used in place of the real thing. Compassion seems much more appropriate than punishment for the people who must live this way.

I am reminded of a woman in a mental institution, rocking back and forth with a doll in her arms that she thought was real. I would not have taken away her doll. I could not give her back her true child who had died many years before. But for the young there is greater hope. There is the real world and the opportunities for genuine fulfilling experiences.

"If you use your own chemical factory, you can experience thrills beyond comprehension," declared Leroy Looper, black therapist and former addict. "Like a great love affair, with somebody you really want to be with. You come to a climax that has never been reached before. There is no pill at the drugstore that can touch that. Or meeting a loved one after many years, and you find yourself crying out of joy."

Belonging

Are you acquainted with the word "esoteric"? It has to do with knowledge and understandings that are limited or restricted to a uniquely initiated special group. Like, "Man, we are in and doin' all this supernatural stuff that is superior to what all those other people are doin', and they are out. They don't know nothin' compared to us."

Esoteric describes the sort of belonging that many people try to attach to membership in drug-oriented groups. Many see belonging to the widely glamorized drug scene as very special. And this, obviously, contributes to drug use.

Some people readily use drugs, at least in part, to feel that they belong to an esoteric group. Some simply see drug use as a requirement of acceptance and to feel that they belong to the groups at hand. The most common social uses of drugs in this country are, of course, those involving legal or "less illegal" drugs. The initially used drugs, as experienced by most people, are cigarettes among friends on the way home from school, beer busts, wine at rap sessions, and the like. And throughout the younger years many adults set the example when good friends get together with coffee and cigarettes in the morning and cocktails later in the day.

Refusing a cigarette or a drink, even if not desired, is very hard those first few times when it seems that everyone else is doing it.

And it is hard to refuse the clearly illegal stuff, unless you have it worked out before the moment of decision arrives.

"It's really hard," a college student who is close to me said when we were talking about it recently. "In some groups, it isn't that they just don't accept you. They reject you. They think you are a narc. They suspect you of being an agent out to get them. The only sensible thing is to find friends that want to go the way you do. It's unbelievable how many dumb mice out there follow along, being drawn into things they really don't want, just because they can't find saving ways to say, 'No.' "

"You have to belong," a young woman in San Francisco told me. "With the pressures I have been under in the last year, there's no way I could have resisted."

"No way." I reflected.

"I really don't think so. 'Course, maybe I wouldn't have the friends I have," she laughed. "But like, when the joint goes around the room and somebody doesn't take it . . . . You know. I don't smoke, and it's really hard for me. But if they're my good friends and they say, 'Good grass,' . . ."

The need to belong can be a powerful force which pulls people in different directions depending on where they are and who they are with at the moment. Much depends on the particular group. Although often neglected, the expectations of straight groups and families to which people wish to belong are factors to be considered in any attempt at decision-making.

After he had been dealing with drug problems as a peace officer in the Berkeley area for a number of years, a friend told me that the only thing he had seen that worked in getting someone off drugs was for the individual to inform on those with whom he had been using drugs. As long as the old crowd still accepted him, this officer believed, there was no end to it.

Everybody needs to belong, and drug use is related in various ways. People are guided to or away from drugs by groups and individuals. But also, some are drawn to use drugs as substitutes for belonging and for the lack of satisfying relationships with groups and caring individuals.

"Drugs open you up without having to open up with another person," said a boy I knew once. "I mean, wow, you open up with somebody, some person, some girl, and she can cut you. Hurt you deep. With people, maybe some you can trust, maybe some. Maybe there is even a girl somewhere. Maybe. But no wonder it comes out that so many boys get this loud, obnoxious front that girls say they don't like. Part of the reason is so guys don't get hurt. Drugs or girls, a risk either way, you know. Some girls are brutal . . . cut you deep . . . then put it on you that a big tough boy is not supposed to feel hurt."

Robert Tucker, a dynamic black Ph.D. from Yale, put it, "If he can't develop a quality relationship with other people, not with objects but with people, there's a very good chance that this kid is going to be one of the individuals who is going to destroy himself. When I talk about destroying himself, I don't differentiate between kids who destroy themselves with speed or heroin or LSD and the kids who commit suicide, or the kid who elects, and I mean *elects*, to become an adolescent schizophrenic."

Tucker stresses the need for alternate need gratification in working with drug problems. Solutions are found, he suggests, in forming relationships with other groups and in developing the capacity to *give* to people rather than just expecting to take.

It may be that a neglected aspect of belonging is in the subtle giving that is so vital in healthy relationships. Our own intelligent input, our own thoughtful, sometimes courageous influence, is often the one thing that can make things better. At precarious times, we reach out to belong when we might instead enable an in-depth belonging to each other.

Voice

Beautiful back-lighted bottles all in a row, psychedelic colors, mystical visions, and the enticing sign that reads, "Don't." The sales pitch for drug culture is everywhere. And the feeble instruction, "Don't," along with the scare tactics of many inadequate drug education courses, cinches the deal for those who like to play anti-establishment games.

Gene M. Smith, a psychologist who recently studied thousands of students from the Boston area, concluded that those who rebel against their teachers and parents are more likely to use alcohol and other drugs. Those least likely, according to his study, are ambitious in regard to schoolwork and cooperative with teachers.

There is little new in such findings—just more verification that drug use is an expression of rebellion. It is another thing people can do that established authority is telling them they should not do, and this automatically makes it something that some people want to do.

Everyone knows people who are consumed by their need to strike out at authority. Their whole life-styles are built around this need. We saw them back in elementary school flashing packs of cigarettes in forbidden places. It is no surprise to see them with a rubber tube and needle in high school, or at least with a sloppier pack of smokes.

For those who are hung up on asserting that they can do what they want and nobody is going to tell them what to do, drug use comes naturally. And, in turn, the consequences come naturally. As with any and all who rebel unintelligently, they find a new master, one more restricting than the one before. In this case, drugs are found to be controlling to the extent that whole lives are dominated by the need to use and maintain supply.

Trying to think realistically of the voice expressed in this mode of rebellion, images come to mind of a man frantically patting pockets in search of a cigarette, the plump housewife taking pills, and the alcoholic taking a bar break to get through the afternoon. And it is depressing to see good minds scrambled and dissociating to the extent that they give loud voice to rejecting the older generation's imperfections and condemning their faults, while all the while following their most ineffectual and destructive examples.

Being Somebody

Doyle did not have the ability to compete in sports or to make grades that were more than barely passing. He was rejected by most of those he wanted as friends. In fact, he was rejected by everyone. Halfway through high school, he moved toward drugs. To meet expenses, he became a supplier, and finally he had people who thought he was somebody from time to time.

When I last heard of Doyle, he was about 20 and had been busted for possession of drugs at a rock concert. But even though he had been arrested and sentenced a number of times before, the boy who saw him after this arrest said, "He was talking it up like he had won some kind of prize. And he was asking people if they had read about him in the papers the last time, when he had a jury trial."

More than a few people reach out for significant identity through drugs. But different people are inclined to be different somebodies, to try to find self-worth in different ways, with the different effects of different drugs. Some, like Doyle, feel they have become important to others in the drug scene. As a brilliant ex-con at Reality House West put it, "He's identifying with something that's, by the media, made so damn glamorous and so esoteric that he can't help but dig it, in his own little sick way."

Others search inwardly for identity, worth, and self-related beauty. Opinions vary as to the validity of discovery through the so-called mind-expanding drugs. I have talked with a few impressively intelligent people who believe they have better feelings about themselves because of drug experiences. And I have talked with some who were so confused that it seemed obvious their emotional insistence on the supremacy of their experiences was defensive autistic restructuring, if not paranoia.

I recall a girl who listened patiently to several people in a group try to top one another by telling of peak experiences in self-discovery through drugs. Finally, she interrupted by saying, "Lots of kids who don't use drugs have worked it out without drugs. They have already found acceptable identity. To them, all this stuff about trying to find yourself through drugs is so much crap. I want to be me, not just some cloud-wandering junky."

At another time, in another place, I remember hearing a counseling psychologist in the Haight-Ashbury talking with a young man who had recently returned from following a mystic. The counselor asked him if he thought drugs were necessary for sensitivity and expansion of consciousness.

"Naw. No, I don't," he answered. "I think that for certain people, like myself, who have been brought up without true values . . . Like I feel I have been more or less taught false values. And I had to use drugs to learn certain consciousness that does exist and always has existed and, I believe, always will exist. On my trip I met several young people who have never taken any psychedelic drugs at all, who have somehow grown up with these values. And I could learn from these people although they had never turned on with drugs." Then, contradicting his initial answer, he said, "But I think drugs are necessary. I think they were just a miracle that came down to help some of us turn on who really needed to turn on."

In contrast, Leroy Looper spoke candidly in recorded conversation: "You take a white kid, coming out of a middle-class bag. And he doesn't particularly like the value system of his time. And he wants to experience something real quick. Instead of being eighteen, he wants to be ninety-nine and get it all at once. You know what I mean? So he goes on one of these quick trips that freaks him out, so he's really ninety-nine, you understand? So he's like a vegetable 'cause he got a bum trip."

In kaleidoscopic ways, the need to be somebody draws many into drug use as a means of imagined prestige, as a supposed tool for psychic discovery, and as an escape from the intolerable feelings of nothingness.

The Look Ahead

People who have not worked at finding adequate fun and fulfillment in life are wide open to experimentation in the multifarious world of perceptual alteration through drugs. And this may seem to help, temporarily. But where's the future in it?

The warning printed on any pack of cigarettes hints at the look ahead for fun patterns that are dependent upon drug use. But those involved are not interested in warning signs. Some take drugs in part because of a lack of optimistic outlooks toward things to come. The bomb, ghettos, energy shortages, pollution, overpopulation, fanatics, deadweight free-loaders, and the lack of trust in leadership contribute to a futile, hopeless outlook. Some people undoubtedly will feel an overwhelming need to play down the importance of this aspect of fun and will develop fantastic rationalizations to avoid awareness of such reality.

It follows that some will argue for fun without a future—pleasure *now*, without the bother or obligations of working for it.

Of course, drugs can provide pleasurable sensations. Drugs are used by medical doctors and advertised on TV as relievers of pain. But their uses are complicated, hard facts of life that all of us must face whether we think of ourselves as a part of the total drug scene or not.

On the top of the list drugs are deceptive. They may relieve the pain and change feelings, but the relief is at best temporary. The world remains, along with its problems and imperfections. Further, the abuse of drugs causes physical and mental damage. There are possible effects on future generations. There are ensnaring dependencies and addictions, both of the physical and psychological varieties.

Still further, the sale and possession of some drugs are against the law. Even though there are arguments against this, it remains the case. And anyone who turns a blind eye to the consequences strikes out when it comes to hope for an optimistic look ahead. Arrests, harassment, confinement in prison, and close association with the underworld—all become a part of your scene once you use illegal drugs.

Most important, there is the question, "Who's tending the store?" While everybody is freaked out, high, escaped to happier places, who's tending the store? Who's making the bread? Who's doing all those things we must have done in order to live? No one can escape the basic law intrinsic in the related concepts of give and take, of production and consumption, of ecological balance, of loving and being loved.

The drug subculture valued or despised, enriching or degrading, exists as a parasite on the straight culture. It is provided for, protected, nurtured, and maintained by the straight culture. It cannot survive without limit and restraint on its growth and the sapping of the straight culture.

We now have a seemingly contradictory situation in this technologically efficient country where it is possible to survive and have a significant measure of freedom without making a corresponding contribution to productivity, at least individually. But there is a limit, perilously undefined and ignored, to the staying power of the straight productive citizens who carry the weight of survival in the world.

There are those who have come to believe that loudly condemning imperfection in others and escaping from reality through drugs can somehow make things better. This is a sickness. But rationalized by leaders of the drug scene, popularized by the media, exploited by profiteers, and ineffectually answered by our lagging institutions, it is a powerful national force. It makes it difficult to turn on to objectivity. It clouds the look ahead.

We cannot afford to let greater and greater segments of our population escape to infantile dependency. It is national suicide. It is the loss of great power and potential in providing the best that humans can offer other humans in this world.

"We are all in this together," is a common cry of enlightenment. And we'd better act like we know it if we want to see good times in the look ahead."

Chapter Sixteen

SEX IS NO FOUR-LETTER WORD

In a previous chapter we noted how our earliest ancestors had basic urges toward aggression and withdrawal. They had fight and flight reactions, or else they would not have lived long enough to be our ancestors. Another basic urge that has continued since the beginning of the human race is sex. An active attraction for the opposite sex was an undeniable trait of our ancestors. Without the urge to procreate and the natural bodily function to make it all happen, we would not be here today.

Sex

Sex has to do with the making of a new life. It has to do with the differences and the relationships between men and women which make new life possible. It has to do with the physical attraction, the emotional feeling, and the thrills which motivate men and women to create life. But by itself, sex offers no guarantee that the new life created will be good or bad. Nor does it insure that the relationships of the people drawn together will be happy or even productive. Sex is blind in these respects. And because of this, regardless of the beauty and the exquisite feelings it may make possible, many people have learned to label it immoral.

Sex is immoral when it causes people to risk creating life that they do not want, life for which they will not accept parental responsibility. It is immoral when it causes children to be conceived who will not be loved or cared for properly, children who will learn to hate. It is immoral when it brings regret, when it is used without intelligence and love.

But there is another side to sex. Sex is moral when it produces children who will be loved and cared for properly. And it is moral when used with intelligence and love.

Sex is a natural function that is subject to the conscious control of the individual. And it may be better to say that sex is neither moral nor immoral. Sex is a basic urge, having the accelerating power to draw people into sometimes moral and sometimes immoral behavior.

Far from applying intelligence to the situation, many teens and as many adults live in a climate of confusion regarding sex. They are ambivalent. They want intensely, but they don't want. They are proud of what they have done sexually, but at the same time, ashamed. They are interested to the point of fascination but believe anything to do with sex is wrong. Lacking a fundamental understanding of sex, they vehemently deny the possibility that there is anything worth knowing that they do not already know.

Some people have been taught by tragic experience or by bitter elders to believe that sex is totally nasty, disgusting, dirty, painful, ugly, degrading, and everything else bad. But still the urge continues in them. And desires and hints of beauty are in sharp contradiction. The resulting explosive conflicts lead to many twisted ideas concerning sex and to many defense mechanisms that are thrown up against realistic views of our evident sexual nature.

A Limited Parallel of Natural Functions

Several ideas may be communicated by drawing parallels between sex and other natural functions. Consider eating, for example.

In prehistoric days, it seems safe to suppose, humans just reached out and grabbed the food available, downing it until their appetites were temporarily satisfied. They ate completely on impulse, when there was food to eat. And when there was not, they ruthlessly hunted it down. They felt like eating, so they ate, with no sensitive thought of sharing. They considered anyone between them and their food to be an enemy. They refused to be delayed. They devoured their food with little thought as to how they might appear to others. They ate for physical satisfaction, devoid of aesthetic pleasure.

Today, most people eat with more restraint. We need food to live, but we control our behavior to answer other needs which are higher in the hierarchy of needs. We wait to eat in accordance with our customs. We care what people think of us when we eat. We have standards of cleanliness. We know that some things are not good for us to eat and that some things make us sick. We enjoy a wholesome pleasure in eating the right foods at the right time and place. We have learned that food tastes better in the right atmosphere and when shared with people we care about and trust. And we know the consequences of disobeying reasonable rules concerning food and eating.

In our complex culture, impulse has had to give way to patterns of restraint. Years of preparation are necessary for responsible adulthood. Early marriage is seldom the best idea. And "free sex" is the most expensive kind.

One increasingly common danger of unrestricted sex is the disenchanting experience of having venereal disease. American teenagers are now being infected at an alarming rate (recently quoted as 1¼ million a year). Without early treatment, VD can cause blindness, possibly eventual insanity, and babies being born deformed. And even with convenient, effective, and relatively confidential treatment (in communities that are enlightened enough to provide such life-or-death service), the whole routine leaves its psychological mark. Attitudes and outlook are never quite the same. (For detailed information and current statistics, consult your library, your local health department, your school nurse, or your counselor.)

In spite of the influence of our very liberal media, of the inferred privilege some college teens read into co-ed living on campus, of a few highly publicized and dramatized alternative life-styles, and of heavy rationalizing all around, advanced expressions of the sex urge outside of marriage are still considered to be wrong by most people.

The parallel between eating and sex can be helpful and valid up to a point. But there are differences, of course. We must eat regularly in order to stay alive. The sex urge lends itself to greater control and to indirect enjoyment and expression.

The Erotic and the Obscene

When something is *erotic*, it tends to arouse sexual love or desire. When something is *obscene*, it tends to disgust. For healthy people, there is a difference.

Erotica are literary or artistic works that tend to sexually arouse people. Obscenities are things that are repulsive to the senses. Again, there is a great difference.

But some people do not see the difference. Tragically, many people are confused about their sexual orientations. Their predispositions or tendencies to respond to sex are about as rational as being prompted to throw up at the sight of a recipe card or being angered by a picture of an appetizing casserole in a home magazine. The beauty or ugliness of things is to a large extent within the eye of the beholder. And this is surely true when it comes to sex.

Of course, it becomes glaringly obvious that it is possible to take the beautiful and picture it as revolting obscenity. To continue the food parallel, that appetizing casserole might be pictured in a garbage can with slop. This brings us close to a reasonable concept of pornography. When a literary or artistic work has the potential of arousing sexual desire but is disgusting, then it rightfully may be called pornography.

Pornography, then, is sexual obscenity. It portrays sex as basically shameful and is commonly associated with violent abuse, obscenities beyond the sexual and destructively misleading acrobatics.

Pornography should be conceptually distinguished from erotic realism, or realistic erotica, which attempts to present honest, sometimes artistic, sometimes romanticized and entertaining portrayals of sexual love.

But the difference between pornography and erotic realism also is in the eye of the beholder. Some people claim that there is no difference whatsoever, and demand that any book, story, picture, painting, movie, TV program, or what-have-you with a sexual theme is automatically pornographic, regardless of the attempted message, beauty, or honesty of presentation.

Pornography

In addition to the controversy over what is pornography and what is not, there is controversy over the probable effects it may have on people and whether, under force of law, we should be prevented from having the relatively indirect experiences that are made available through sex-oriented materials.

In 1967, the Congress of the United States created a commission to "study the effects of obscenity and pornography upon the public, and particularly minors, and its relationship to crime and other antisocial behavior. . . ." The commission's research extended into 1970 and cost well over $1,000,000.

It was verified, for example, that "first experience with explicit sexual materials usually occurs in adolescence. . . . Roughly 80% of boys and 70% of girls have seen visual depictions or read textual descriptions of sexual intercourse by the time they reach age 18. . . ."

Although the commission revealed no surprises, its findings were extensive. The following is only a sampling from the commission's majority report:

"People with more education are more likely to have experience with erotic materials . . . . There is some suggestion that young people who are less active socially are less likely to be acquainted with sexual materials. . . . Surveys of psychiatrists, psychologists, sex educators, social workers, counselors, and similar professional workers reveal that large majorities of such groups believe that sexual materials do not have harmful effects on either adults or adolescents. On the other hand, a survey of police chiefs found that 58% believed that 'obscene' books played a significant role in causing juvenile delinquency . . . . Experimental and survey studies show that exposure to erotic stimuli produces sexual arousal in substantial portions of both males and females . . . . Exposure to erotic stimuli appears

to have little or no effect on already established attitudinal commit-
ments regarding either sexuality or sexual morality . . . . Delinquent
and nondelinquent youth report generally similar experiences with
explicit sexual materials . . . . Available research indicates that sex
offenders have had less adolescent experience with erotica than other
adults . . . ."

It is noteworthy that a number of law enforcement officials are
quoted who repeatedly find sexual materials in the possession of
sexual offenders. There seems no way of knowing, however, the
cause and effect relationship or to what extent sexual materials
actually enable people with otherwise inadequate outlets to cope
with sexual pressures without committing an offense against another
person.

Pictures of banks and stories about holdups may be in the possession of robbers, and pictures of important people and stories about
them may be in the possession of assassins. But such pictures and
stories in the hands of hundreds of thousands of other people does
not make them suspect—even though most people, with or without
the materials, have secretly fantasied get-rich robberies and murder-
ing their powerful enemies.

As for confessions, a sex offender scapegoating books and motion
pictures for his or her crime comes off with all the scientific validity
of Flip Wilson's old bit with Geraldine claiming, "The devil made
me buy that dress."

Beyond the statistics and experienced opinions, it remains fair to
state that the impact of erotic and obscene materials is different on
different people. Some people are aroused by shoes, underwear,
bananas, socks, perfume, soft beds, and gentle words.

Censorship? By Whom?

A number of people (of all ages) find a terrible threat to their
self-picture in the normal tendency to think and fantasize about
sex. To them it seems totally unacceptable to think such things or be
tempted to look at pornographic or even mildly erotic items. In defense, they slip to a reaction formation and believe that their feelings are the opposite of what they truly are.

These people may view or read material muttering, "Shameful . . . filth," while deep inside they are enjoying themselves with their "socially acceptable" opportunity to see what there is to see. They may have no definable criteria. They may know only that some books and materials seem shocking and therefore should be prohibited from viewing by anyone else—after they themselves have looked them over, to pass judgment.

A comedian who I couldn't stomach as a rule came through with a bit I had to listen to a few years ago. It was about a father who had taken his children to a movie that turned out to be an erotic film. He had them cover their eyes and angrily took them from the theater. But before the father realized the picture was X-rated, his monologue went something like this: "Hey, here comes a good part. See his hands are creeping toward her neck. He's going to strangle his wife, I'll bet. He's going to kill her. Then guess how he's going to do away with the body? Oh my! What's this? Why he's unbuttoning her blouse. Now he's touching her breasts. What kind of a filthy thing is this? I thought it was a G-rated picture. Don't look. Don't look. He's making love to her."

The target of most anti-smut people is not obscenity but sex. Vicious obscenity—both in language and violence—seems to be allowed until sexual exposure enters in. That normal human bodies in the act of making love should be considered so offensive that there are laws in this country which would deny such scenes even to adult audiences, while acts of killing and war are readily available to all ages, tells something about our confusion.

Actually, the pornographer and the would-be censor have much in common. Both distort the true, healthy nature of sex. Both try to make ugly something intended to be beautiful. Both mislead people and create attitudes that can interfere with normal expressions of sex. It remains the task of individual people who seek happiness and satisfaction in their lives to be their own sexual managers and, as intelligently as possible, to pick and choose their own experiences, whether vicarious or direct.

Chapter Seventeen

IT OUGHT TO BE FUN

The satisfaction of any and all biological needs follows a basic sequence:

1. Drive to answer the current need results in tension and physical preparation of the body to perform the appropriate natural function.
2. Activity is directed toward a goal-object that is believed to have the potential of providing satisfaction.
3. Gratification of the biological need results in *pleasurable* sensations as tension and drive are reduced.

Maximum pleasure as a part of need gratification is important to us all—pleasure that should be experienced from the physical sensations and from the satisfaction of related psychological needs. Psychological needs are closely associated with biological needs. They often overlap and are hard to distinguish. In the healthy person within a healthy environment, one should not contradict the other. When ambivalence and conflict must accompany bodily satisfactions, both psychological and physical problems tend to develop.

Small babies whose mothers are unwilling to hold them and make feeding time a loving time, for example, may learn lasting feelings that the world is a cold, unfriendly place and that they are unworthy of being loved. The teenager whose dinner hour means family quarrels, angry criticisms, and stuffing the food down as fast as possible to get away from the table lives in a different world from those who leisurely enjoy meals and pleasant conversation about mutual concerns with people who show that they truly care about one another.

Having a happy life is obviously impossible if the natural functions of the body are associated with discomfort, anger, guilt, or fear. Sex is no exception. It may be many things to different people. But for everyone, it ought to be *fun*.

Apply the Formula

Sex differs from all other natural functions in that it is the one that can be most controlled. Unlike breathing, eating, or going to the toilet, acting to directly fulfill sexual functions may be postponed, indefinitely.

The look ahead. Intelligent control and the postponement of advanced sexual activity are necessary in order to gain the greatest possible pleasure and continuing, long-lasting opportunities for fun. Pre-marital experiences are usually awkward and handicapped at best. They often require very limited personal commitment, when there ought to be total devotion. Deceptions and suspicions are common. Feelings of guilt and a desire to break away may dominate, when there ought to be feelings of joy and the expectations of new and better things to come, together throughout life.

Initial moments have a way of being final. First impressions count. And initial sexual experiences have impact on future attitudes and feelings. Where you first find sexual thrills and physical orgasmic satisfactions, happily or unhappily, you will likely return in reality and in fantasy many times in your future.

Action. Sex is there for each individual to work out in the ways that seem right and best for him or her. Acts that risk disease, ties with destructive people, or the conception of unwanted children are more than foolish, of course, regardless of the rationalizations some use to try to excuse behavior. Vicarious experiences, alternatives to penetration, sublimations, and masturbation are readily available and matters of personal decision. But know yourself and the self you will be tomorrow, after the tensions have subsided, and do not violate your personal taboos. Guard against letting the inertia of the going action bringing you to share orgasmic experiences with people you will not want to remember with closeness.

Discovery. The possibilities of learning and discovery in sex are many, and perhaps they are made even more intriguing by the teasing obstacles in the game. Books and erotica inform and misinform. Observing, listening, rapping with friends and relatives, and experiencing the functions of one's own body add more. Then eventually, there comes the opportunity to discover physical sharing with another human being. But at any stage of our education, we are liable to have a problem in not realizing what we do not yet know about sex.

"I am thinking," a boy told me during a time of discovery, "that if you really care enough for a girl that you would want to spend your entire life with her, you would want to have peak experiences with her that you would know she has never had with anyone else. Just yours, you know? And I'm not talking double standard. It should be the same for the man as for the woman. So they could unfold sex together. Of course, I have messed myself up on this. And so has the girl I am going with now, I know. But I can see that's the way I wish it could be, now."

Or as a girl was told by an older sister, "So sure. Go ahead and invent the wheel all over again. Lots of people do. But I wish you could learn by seeing and maybe be happier than I am with my life."

Emotional experiences. The emotional experiences of sex undeniably top the list of functions and activities that may be considered fun—unless ambivalences and conflicts, conscious or unconscious, take too much away; and, of course, unless somewhere along the hierarchy of needs there are other natural functions that override and dominate the moment. Not having had any food or water for a couple of days, being suffocated, wanting to escape intense pain, or having to go to the toilet could surely take the fun out of it. But as a rule, sex is so much fun that some will take reasonable exception to my calling it *fun* instead of ecstacy, rapture, or transport, or to quote theologian Dr. Urban T. Holmes III, an Episcopal priest, "Sexual union is, in fact, a glimpse of heaven."

It is not just the final orgasm or the release of tension that is enjoyed, no more than in eating do we only enjoy the moment our hunger is completely satisfied. The state of emotional excitement and certainly the sensations of stimulation are to be enjoyed. Still, emotional states are preparations for an act, in this case, for sexual intercourse and for the attempted fertilization of the ovum. And substitute activities, compensatory alternatives, or intended prohibitions against extended stimulation should be worked out in advance by anyone who does not wish to be drawn into sexual intercourse.

Sex is subject to individual control. You can be angry and not attack in this civilized world. You can suffer fear and not run away. And you can be sexually aroused and not have sexual intercourse. But it helps to think things through before moments of decision.

Belonging. Sex can provide a closeness which can make people feel that they belong like they have never belonged before. But it is not to be entered into reluctantly, against a person's better judgment, just in order to belong. The fun comes when there is a future in it. The grandest sensations turn into despair when it turns out that there really was no belonging to the act after all and that the partner only sought physical release and claims a life-style of belonging to no one.

Voice. Sex is truly fun when it is what you want to do. It can be terrifying or depressing if it is happening against your will. Your voice in whether or not, and what, how, where, and with whom, can make all the difference in whether it is fun or not. You are responsible for your own body and for whether or not sexual activities turn out to be enjoyable for you. Merely handing over the controls to someone else is risky business. Sex is something you enter into because you want to and feel that it is right for you, never because you are pressured into it and never out of rebellion, or because those in authority say they do not want you to and they think it is wrong.

"Well, I wouldn't have done it. I sure wouldn't have gone all the way with him. Not with him. But I'd had a big hassle with my parents that night, and this was my way of getting back." Doing what one feels like doing and then scapegoating others is sick.

Being somebody. "Don't ask me to turn off George. I was nothing till he came along."

There is a feeling of identity that comes with a loving sexual experience. It can mean unsurpassed self-discovery. The question arises, however, as to who it is you become through your sexual experience. Your values and your ideas about the person you want to be are important. When sex helps you be and become what you want to be, it is fun. When it draws you into self-deprecation and keeps you from being the person you want most to be, it can be hell.

Worthy identity in our own eyes and in the eyes of others has to do with sexual conduct and with sexuality—*sexuality* being the manner in which we assert and become members of our own sex. We are all sexual beings. Women are women in many, quite different ways. Men are men in many, quite different ways. And women and men come together as sex partners in many, quite different ways. The societal limitations on how we become and gain feelings of worthy identity are fewer than ever before.

Within these expanded dimensions there are fantastic opportunities for fun. But there are pitfalls and false prophets. With new freedom comes responsibilities incomprehensible to some. And the happiest of times are reserved for those who understand and care.

Bonds of Love and Sex

The prime purpose of sex is creation of life. But as surely as there are reason and order under God and nature, the purpose of sex is more than this. A human child needs more than to be given breath. A child needs parental care in the early years of life. Sex has a part in building relationships that keep couples together and make possible the care and counsel necessary for the healthy upbringing of the young. Sex fosters and fortifies love.

Every person with whom you have a sexual experience becomes a part of you, of your self-structure, in a special way that you can never escape. As many people have discovered, these emotional ties are not magically dissolved by marriage to someone else. Nor are they dissolved when a so-called liberated individual decides to break away and switch partners. The bonds persist in varied, subtle ways, both within the thoughts of the individual and beyond, in the thoughts of new and old partners.

Bonds of friendship can continue without conflict, but not bonds formed by sexual intimacy. Sexual experiences bring lasting happiness when shared with one you love, with one to whom you have a lasting commitment. You lower your chances for happiness when you create ties that must be broken, when you form relationships that must be betrayed, when you have intense emotional experiences that must be somehow rationalized away.

We all know of people who believe in moving around. And if we really know them, we inevitably see them tied to someone to whom they do not want to be tied.

"Wow, I wish she would stop calling me. We agreed to split. I don't want to hurt her, but I care a lot about the new girl, now. I'm really serious about this one." Or, "And I want it to be perfect and beautiful and sacred with my husband. I do. And then fantasies start flooding my mind of the times with Hank, and I feel rotten and guilty and just want to die . . ." Or, "She and I more or less slept together weekends the first quarter of our sophomore year in college. Then according to our agreement, she started trying out other guys. We were both to have complete freedom. But it is tearing me apart. Like I wouldn't have believed it could."

"After all, it's a new, free, liberated world," some tell us. "There's the pill and all that. So there's no real risk involved."

But there are many risks. In any setting, with any person, the willingness to have sex with another person always involves a willingness to be physically and emotionally vulnerable to the acts of that person. In marriage there is calculated risk. In "free love" there is often uncalculated risk.

Sex is not always related to what we think of as love. It can be linked with hate. It is not expressed by everyone through tenderness and affection. It is expressed by some through hostility and painful aggression.

People are different. They have somewhat different needs. They have been taught differently about sex and love. They have experienced different things—both happy and unhappy. And people differ physically. But the tendency for sex to form ties persists, regardless of the differences and in spite of the confusion created by misinformation, guilt feelings, and conflict. Sex builds bonds between people. And in marriage or out, being tied to someone you do not love is a terrible limitation on fun.

Chapter Eighteen

LOVES

"I know I love him," she said, peering out the window. "But I don't know if I really do. We have fun together, anyway. And then, I have my moments when I know I love everyone, in a kind of global way."

Loves are varied and many, and they are hard to communicate. All attempts at definitions fall short.

What Is Love?

On one thing we should be able to agree. Love is an attraction we feel for some person, object, or idea. And why are we attracted to something? Because we feel a need for it. We may not know exactly why we need it, but the feeling is in us that we do.

Two people in love feel a need for each other. People who stay in love feel a continuing mutual satisfaction of needs. Love itself is a need. In addition, love is linked with every other need. We show our love for others by trying to understand and provide for their needs. We receive love when someone feels we can satisfy his or her needs. We need people when we love them. We love them when we need them. We are needed because we are loved. And we are loved because we are needed. The hierarchy of needs, then, can help conceptualize the how and why of love. People having different needs tend to love for different reasons.

In some parts of the world where people exist on the bare

necessities of life, a woman may come to love a man because he gives her food, and a man may come to love a woman because she works hard in the fields. But very few of us worry about where our next meal is coming from. The needs we feel for security, status, intellectual growth, happiness, and purpose in life have more to do with determining whom we love than does the basic hunger need.

Among teens in our culture there is just one commonly frustrated biological need—sex. As a result, sex becomes an active need seeking expression. And right or wrong, good or bad, sex is an influential element in our unconscious choice of whom we will love and in our selection of a lifelong mate.

Skin-Deep Love

Beauty is another word that is difficult to define. We experience it in many ways. We see it, hear it, and feel it deep within us. We sense it with throbbing sensations and a tingling up the spine. We share it with those we love. But sometimes what we see as beauty causes us to be misled in love.

Beauty is something we must *learn* to recognize and appreciate. This is especially true of the skin-deep beauty of the opposite sex. Each culture creates its own picture of what is a beautiful woman and a handsome man. Skim a few anthropology books for examples of what some groups have sincerely believed was beauty in their young ladies, and you will get an idea of the continuing joke we human beings play on ourselves. Designs of scars on face and body, missing front teeth, immense obesity, stretched lips and ear lobes, and hair decorated with mud have made girls beautiful to their men in some parts of the world. The trim figure, eye makeup, and our current hair styles seem as silly to millions of people in cultures other than our own. We are taught our ideas of beauty. And herein lies one of the greatest obstacles to love and genuine happiness for the teens of today.

We have been educated to believe that beauty and love come in rather specific packages—the images created by the fiction of literature, movies, retouched pictures, and TV. We develop a mental picture of the ideal face and measurements of the opposite sex. But as things work out, the package with the most attractive wrappings may contain the least. It may be the least likely to provide the intelligent company, the fun, or the eventual deep love we want and seek.

The Power of Love

I have suggested that we express love by answering the needs of those we love. We help provide them with food and water if this is what they need. We protect them if their survival is threatened. We help them to gain self-respect or to grow intellectually. This is all a part of caring. But never forget that an important need is for love itself. Every person needs to know that there is someone who genuinely cares. The world can seem a very threatening place—full of conflicts, name-callers, competitors, and rejecting people who constantly remind us of our shortcomings and make us feel much less than we want to be. It can seem an inconsistent, unfair, and lonely place. We all need emotional support from someone.

Disturbed or threatened people (and we are all disturbed or threatened from time to time) feel rejected and unaccepted. They find it difficult to function with such feelings. The need to eliminate the threat of rejection is felt much more keenly than any self-actualization need or even the need for self-respect. It is more basic in the scale of the hierarchy of needs.

The answer to this persistent need is love—the love of another person (or, for those who know it to be so, the love of God). This is a love of acceptance, not a love that somehow tolerates or demands changes, but a love that accepts a person as he or she is. Acceptance, which should be a part of both brotherly and romantic love, can push back the threats and make it possible to sense the need for self-respect and self-actualization. It can make a person want to be successful. It can enable a despairing person to live and think deeply and to find happiness.

Love Is Meant to Flow Two Ways

"Man, she loves me like I don't exist," a boy aptly said of his pert little girl friend. "I mean, she wants everything her way. She's got a couple of other boys around. And that's OK. We aren't going steady or anything. But she gets sore when I pay attention to other girls. I mean, she takes but doesn't know how to give."

Some teens, and some adults I know, are misers when it comes to love. They try to get all they can, but they do not want to give. Never seeming to have enough love and attention, they live miserable lives. They have not learned the simple fact that love worth having must flow in more than one direction.

There is as great a satisfaction in the giving as in the receiving. If you doubt this, ask yourself whether you would rather be married to a person you love who doesn't love you or to a person you don't love who does love you. Obviously, you don't want either situation. You want both to love and to be loved. You want the feeling to be mutual.

As the people you care about help to answer your needs, you must help to answer theirs. There should be a healthy balance.

"Be a good listener," we are told, for example. But a healthy relationship requires more than this. Don't just give attention. See that you get some in return. In a conversation you owe it to anyone you care for to speak as well as listen, to take as well as give. This stimulates growth. Work toward a balanced, two-directional flow with anyone you care about. You both will be better for it. And if you love, your love becomes a deeper love. Some seas are dead and some ponds stagnant because water flows only into them and never out.

One and Only

"Somewhere in this world there is the one just meant for me. The one and only. The one for whom I am the only one. And it is our destiny some day to meet and love and marry."

I wouldn't want to try to talk anyone out of this bit of fantasy. I find myself subscribing to it in my more romantic moments. But as a counselor and an observer of life, I cannot buy it. I have seen it hurt too many people.

I remember Jeanette, who loved a boy who didn't love her, no matter what she did to win his love (and she did too much). She went on for many bitter months and years carrying her painful torch, convinced in fantasy that he was the one and only boy she could ever love. At long last, Jeanette dated another boy and found very soon that the first love suffered by comparison to the new one.

When for any reason a love relationship between two people ends, or when it is longed for and never gets started, the situation is sad, indeed. But this does not have to be the end of love. There can be other, greater loves for those courageous enough to let them happen.

There is no one and only person you can love any more than there is one and only vocation in which you can be successful. Unsuccessful loves do not necessarily mean that future loves will fail any more than unsuccessful business ventures mean that future ventures will fail. You can learn from your experiences. Mistakes and misfortune can increase your understanding and intensify your joys and successes when they finally arrive.

It may be that, in theory as well as in fantasy, there is one who can best answer your personal needs. But there are many who might do a very satisfactory job of answering these needs and, therefore, many with whom you could share a deep and satisfying love.

Of course, the fact that there can be more than one love in your life can cause you trouble. I remember Shirley, who dreamed of one true, perfect love. A dozen times she told herself she had finally found the one she longed for. But two of these times she was already married to someone else. Now, in her third marriage, she has moods when she is convinced that her first husband must have been her one and only love, and she is sorry she did not stay with him. She says her present husband must not be right for her because she is still attracted to other men.

Not even a marriage ceremony can keep you from feeling attraction for more than one member of the opposite sex. These attractions are natural. But there is nothing fatally lacking in your love for one person just because you feel attracted to someone else. The old love does not have to be replaced by a new one each time this happens.

You can love more than once. And you can love more than one

person at the same time. Obviously, this does not always lead to perfect contentment. But it need not lead to disaster, either. The endless maze of destructive conflicts can be avoided. It is hard to do sometimes, but stay clear of people you are attracted to if you do not want to risk falling in love and developing sexual bonds.

Your chances of experiencing lasting love do not hang on finding the fictional or theoretical one and only in the world for you. They depend on your capacity to narrow the field to one and one only—to just one person with whom you seek fulfillment and on this person's capacity to do the same with you.

Women's Rights, Men's Rights, and Wrongs

"The trouble with boys," a girl once told me, "is that they have this dumb picture of what a boy is supposed to be—big and strong and all that junk. But the worst, the very worst, is that thing that gets going with some of them that they have to see how far they can go with a lot of different girls. And then, as if that wasn't awful enough, they think they have to brag about it, trying to prove what big men they are because of it."

I commented that not all boys had this attitude.

"I should hope not," she said. "Who would want them? As a date or anything? Can you imagine what it would be like for a girl, falling for a boy like that? Or being married to him? How could a girl love him or feel he loved her, knowing that making love was just sport for him? And knowing he was maybe thinking of a half dozen other girls or comparing. Or knowing he might pick up his old habits any time he got bored. I want a boy who's mine as much as I'm his." She stared off into space a while and said, "Girls are different from each other, I guess."

The inevitable response of a number of girls has been more human than wise.

"You want to know the real reason I got into lib?" another explained. "Sure, we are trying to do some good things politically and I believe in all that, too. But I was really hit by the idea that if the men are going to sleep around, why isn't it just as right for the women? It enraged me, and it still does, for a man to think that it is all right to have sex with all the women he feels like but, even with the pill and contraceptives, that it is evil for a woman to have any sex at all. I decided I wanted part of the action."

Another time, another place, this same woman gave me her dramatic definition of love: "Love is what you do just a little while before you start to hate."

The pain of past mistreatment and rejection is bound to bring on defensive attitudes.

Liberation from a phony, rationalized double standard? No argument. Liberation to strike back in revenge for mistreatment? Understandable. Even liberation from prohibitions against rough sports and combat duty? Fair play. But liberation from commitment in affairs of love? Disastrous!

Love and expressions of love make people so totally vulnerable to each other that commitment is absolutely indispensable—if it is to be more than "what you do just a little while before you start to hate."

The Fun of Loving

OK. The *joy* of loving. The *ecstacy*. The *thrill* and *wonder* of it. No matter what, the formula applies.

Action. Please do not sit there agonizing like some inhibited, confined Victorian clod. Show that you care about people. Reach out a hand. Act with intelligent control, but do something.

Discovery. Since love makes you vulnerable to hurt, try to learn what you can vicariously and by observing the scene. But it cannot all be learned secondhand. Discover the fun of actively caring by helping to answer the genuine needs of people.

Emotional experiences. Let go and know the feeling and sensations—but with forethought to the accelerating power of emotions and with planned safeguards so you will not be carried where you know you do not want to go.

Belonging. To some "possession is nine tenths of the love." Others might be more inclined to declare, "Nobody, but nobody, owns me.

I can walk away from this any time I please." But in the best relationships, there is a feeling of belonging to each other and/or to the universe that approaches oneness, an eternal unity that transcends disagreements.

Voice. Let your lover and loved ones know what you like and don't like. If they love, they will try to please and will want the best for you. And if you love, use part of your active voice to seek what they like and don't like in return.

Being somebody. Be a somebody who counts through commitment. And see that partners recognize your significance and worth through their commitment to you.

The look ahead. Think about acts of love enough so that things both done and undone will bring a minimum of future regrets and a maximum of future happiness. Being realistic places no restriction on happiness. Creative realism enhances the chances of fulfillment.

Plan and prepare. Work at it. Nothing as great as love comes for nothing.

In the vicarious world of fiction, a love of thrills and comfort can conquer any problem. In real life the love required is called *work,* and even this does not do the job unless it is skillfully and intelligently accomplished. But the satisfactions and the anticipations can make the whole thing fun.

Chapter Nineteen

THE TIME OF YOUR LIFE

People tell us, "Life is what we make it." But this is true only up to a point. Anne Frank, for example, made life about as good as she could. But we would have wished much better for her. Fate and circumstances beyond our control play a substantial part in shaping our lives.

There is more useful truth in the maxim, "Energy is where you put it." We may not control our circumstances as much as we would like. But we can decide where we will apply our energies.

Rebel with Cause

Teenagers are, by nature, rebels with powerful, potentially explosive energies. The fact that teens tend to rebel is not in itself bad. If we did not start to strike out on our own in our teens, we would still be dependent on our parents when we are 40. A certain amount of conflict and resistance to authority is natural in every home, school, and community where there are teens.

So rebel! Follow the examples of the great revolutionists who started this country. Exercise the *voice* this book refers to as a necessary component of fun in life. But let it be a rebellion that accomplishes something of value. Improve on what has gone before.

Too many so-called rebellions are only loud noises. They are nothing more than aggressive reactions to frustration or childish examples of scapegoating—"getting even with my folks because they won't buy me a cycle," or "hittin' the establishment because they don't take care of me like they should."

Rebel with just cause. Pick up something that can go somewhere. Rebel against poverty and ignorance in our country and around the world. Opportunities are available through your government and elsewhere for the use of all the energy you can muster—both in the preparation for such service and in actually doing the job.

Rebel against the lack of enthusiasm for learning that you may find around you. Do not be stopped from achieving in school or from asking questions by the do-nothing pressures of the crowd, if you have the misfortune to be in such a crowd. When the able-minded young of this country simply loaf instead of learn it is a very real threat to us all.

Rebel against the attitude that people should not cooperate with the enforcement of laws designed for our protection and the preservation of our liberties. Rebel against the lack of respect shown the symbols of our country. For some people these have become more symbolic of the way they feel about themselves.

Rebel against your elders when they do not set the reasonable examples they should. "Respect your elders," we are told. But which elders? Some may owe us more respect than we owe them.

The nature of modern rebellion is crucial, however. And violence is a cop out. Constant hassle is little better. You cannot expect perfection from anyone. Picking away at minor human errors is a waste. Energies are better expended on trying to work out what better things you can offer. Attack brings more defenses of the sort that prompted the rebellion in the first place. Objects of justified rebellion are already confused, frustrated, defensive people. It is the old frustration-aggression cycle over and over again. Rebellion ought to bring something better. If it does not, then what's the point?

Remember the Law

Arguments related to drugs and the laws restricting their use are as varied as the needs, experiences, and life-styles of the different people who are arguing. It can be argued, for example, that if drugs are really bad, then punishment comes automatically, as a natural consequence of their use. There is no need to pound on the people who use them. The need is to help users find better ways, more satisfactory outlets, not to compound their problems. The punishment of pushers and suppliers may be reasonable; but the further punishment of victims is little more than institutionalized sadism, this argument goes.

It can be argued that some drugs serve illuminating and recreational purposes far outweighing the risks involved, and that those who think so should be left alone. A number of drugs are already legalized, it is argued, and even though there are recognized harmful effects, society has not collapsed as a result.

It can be argued that get-tough laws and intensified attacks on the sources of supply only raise the cost of drugs, and that the underworld will always find a way when the profits are high. High cost, it is further argued, forces users into crimes of robbery, burglary, and prostitution in order to support their habits.

Many people also believe that all laws against drug use should be abolished. There are many points of view. I recall a girl telling of her brother saying to her, "Stay out of it. It's none of your business. If the guy wants to become a vegetable, that's his own concern." But is it? Is it just the user's concern when there are people who care?

Another argument contends that when anyone in society drops out, an added load is placed on the rest of us, a totally unfair load. It might be "his business" if it did not affect others, like a girl friend or a mother. But when he becomes a dead-weight dependent or hurts other people, it is clearly more than just his own concern. And when he is viewed as a member of society, everyone is a victim.

Drug use, inevitably, becomes more than a matter for individual decision. And just as inevitably, groups are going to attempt to cope with their group problems through the development and the enforcement of laws. Imperfect though the system may be, it exists, with prisons and the whole bit. No drug-cloud fantasies will wish it away. Working through the system to replace current laws with better ones always makes sense. But ignoring the existence of the laws now in force or rationalizing that it is all right to violate the laws because they are not fair can bring fun to an abrupt halt.

"Rightsibilities"

A number of years ago I asked a prison psychologist what he thought ought to be stressed most in working with teens. His answer was one of urgent concern and conviction. "Teach them to stand on their own two feet," he said. "Nothing is more important. In that great stone fortress where I work, there are hundreds of confused and dangerous men. There are many thousands more like them across the country, both in and out of prison. Now, we psychologists dream up different names for different types of criminals, but basically, there is only one thing wrong with them, only one reason why it is necessary to keep them locked up. This reason is *they never learned to stand on their own two feet.* They never got past the infantile attitude that the world owes them a living. Most of them know right from wrong, but they seem helpless to do anything about it.

"These monstrous babies still have the idea that if they are hungry, someone should be expected to come along and feed them, that if they are uncomfortable or if they have dirtied themselves, someone should come and make them all comfortable and clean again. And if this does not happen, if they don't get what they want without exerting themselves, they feel the world is being unfair, and they feel justified in lashing out and hurting people and in taking things which aren't theirs. They believe they have rights without obligations or responsibilities."

Perhaps we should invent a new word—"rightsibilities." Rights and responsibilities are only different aspects of the same thing. The right to vote is a responsibility. The right to drive is a responsibility. The right to love and make love is a responsibility. The right to an education is a responsibility. The right to work is a responsibility. The free world of tomorrow will be great or meager, fun-filled or dismal, stable or just plain nonexistent, as we and others cause it to be. What it is becoming depends on how we choose to use our rights—our "rightsibilities."

To Those Who Have It Rough

So you think you have it rough. Some teens do. For some it has been a grossly unfair world from many points of view. And this can put some limitations on having fun.

What is it to have it rough? Using the concepts presented in this book, it is a matter of not having your needs met as well as you believe they should be. And this takes us again to the nature of needs. Much depends on where you are in the hierarchy of needs. The deciding question is not, "Are your basic biological and safety needs being met?" It is, *"Are the needs you sense and feel being met, no matter what they may be?"* When the most urgent and demanding of these needs are being met, you feel that you are having it good. When they are not, you feel that you are having it rough.

By this explanation, you may have all your basic biological and safety needs satisfied completely and still feel that you are having it so rough that it is unbearable. If you sense a need for love or for self-respect, for example, and are constantly unsuccessful in finding an answer to this need, life may seem just as rough for you as it is for someone in need of food. And in such a case, your behavior may appear desperate.

At first glance, it might seem inconceivable that rich and powerful people ever lack for fun. But wealth and power are not on the fun-formula list. There are well-to-do people who seem to have everything anyone could want to make them happy but who are frantic or depressed because they are not quite able to reach what they feel they want most. Beautiful screen stars have been known to commit suicide. Wealthy businessmen have been known to embezzle. Obviously, unhappiness and lack of satisfaction are not reserved for the poverty-stricken.

When considering the varied needs different people feel, we have awesome reminders "that all men are created equal" and stand equal under God in very subtle ways. Regardless of rank and income, there is an equalizer at work in the feelings and needs of human beings. There are general principles that apply to us all.

Imperfect as the ways of the Bushman and the Australian aborigine may be from our civilized points of view, perhaps we can learn from them. Although it is difficult to measure, these people seem to feel happier than many of us who "enjoy" the blessings of modern conveniences. How could this be?

For one reason, they live with a much simpler need structure. That is, their lives are built around more basic needs. They do not count on cities full of material things that they feel are absolutely necessary to their existence. More than this, they appreciate and make the most of what they have. They learn how to live effectively with their world, rather than fighting it because they imagine it to be unfair. They do what they know must be done to survive, instead of being angry because someone else is not doing it for them. Superstitious and unsanitary though they may be, they understand their world better than most of us understand ours. They recognize the consequences of not going along with their morality.

Roughing it now and then in the great outdoors can be a valuable experience in learning what life is all about. Some teens have been so sheltered that they do not know what it is like to be bad off, except from an opulently subjective point of view. Many teens do not know what it is like to be hungry or to be really tired from long, hard work or from a mountain hike.

Having had it a bit rougher than usual can help you appreciate what you have. It awakens feelings of the more basic needs and provides perspective. This explains, in part, how millions of young people have been helped to grow up through experiences in rugged outdoor activities, in hospital work, or in the armed forces.

An old man, short on schooling and long on wisdom, once told me, "Thinkin' on what you ain't been through yourself is like tryin' to come from where you ain't never been." And there is a distinct advantage in having had it rough when it comes to thinking about life in general and about needs in particular. The person who has had it rough and has overcome more than his share of obstacles to achieve success gains much in the process.

Remember Booker T. Washington's "advantage of disadvantages"? Having had it rough can turn out to be one of the biggest advantages you can have in life. Wanting something better than you have had can drive you on to success. And having had it rough can enable you to appreciate that something better once you get it.

If You Are Lucky Enough to Grow Old

"Is it necessary to become cynical and cranky as you grow old?" one of my students in a summer psychology class asked me. "Do you have to stop having fun?"

"I hope not," I told her.

"I hate to think of becoming like some of the old people I know," she said. "It's bad enough when the body starts going to pot, but when you start being down on everything, giving up hope and faith—it must be rotten."

Another student broke in to say, "This doesn't just happen to old people. It happens to us. Lots of kids I know let themselves go to pot. They booze it up and stuff. And they couldn't care less."

"That's not the same," said someone else.

"But the traps of life are similar," I said. "For example, inevitably, every person who manages to live long enough discovers that material possessions are of very limited worth, and so are status and fame, and popularity.

"You, too, may be lucky enough to grow old and look back and ask yourself, 'Was it worth the trip? What did I accomplish of lasting value? What was the point of it all?' "

Live so there are answers you will want to hear. Live with purpose. My guess is that the same teenager who moans today, "There's nothing to do in this town," will cry tomorrow, "There's just no fun in life for me. I never had the breaks," and then in later years, "Nobody cares about us old folks."

Contrast this with the person who keeps an eye to the future and who forces purpose into his life. Purposes are all around us. The fun formula can help with their accomplishment. And for those who want a full life and are willing to exert themselves to find it, there are optimistic years ahead.

But no enchanted waving of wands can make old people happy

and content—any more than an eighteenth birthday or a marriage ceremony can guarantee "happiness forever after." A full old age is just another step in a full life.

Live so that when there are regrets, they are because the great adventure on earth is drawing to a close, not because of things undone, unsaid, unaccomplished, and unworthy. Applying the seventh component of the fun formula to these later years, you can use intelligence to find your own personal answers to the questions, "What of mine will live after me?" and "What lies ahead?"

Our Very Human Future

At times I have a rather human reaction to the popular practice of describing hurtful experiences and faulty institutional systems as "dehumanizing." It is the wrong word to use, it seems to me. With the meaning intended, we might as aptly say, "humanizing." The nature of a lot of humans just is not all that good. Some very human humans have done some terrible things.

Accepting the human bond among us, *we humans* have destroyed. We have killed one another viciously. We have tortured with the rationalizations of supposed morality. Yet, we have saved life. We have invented medicines, discovered ways to ease suffering, and reached for better ways together. We have loved.

We are contradictory animals. The good and the bad become confused in us. We show greatness, then become enslaved by petty points of view that are not even intelligently selfish. We strive for fun, then do things which make it impossible.

It has been the position of this book that much of our difficulty stems from the fear of looking at ourselves as we really are. To the extent that this is true, our hope may come through closer recognition of our nature as fellow human beings. We are the product of heredity and environment. We are the product of our circumstances. But we are more. Equipped with a brain having a large frontal lobe, we are capable of complex thought. We are capable of reason. And we are capable of deep and lasting love.

Here then, is what sets us apart from the lower animals—our

superior potential for reason and love. The degree to which we use and develop this potential, we are people. The degree to which we do not, we are mere human animals—doomed to extinction as other animals before us.

We have cause to look ahead and think. We have the capacity to know the threats to our survival. And the well-being of tomorrow rests heavily on the soundness of the fun we seek to enjoy today.

I found a poster in bright psychedelic style that read, *"Today was made for you."* It is a happy, fun-oriented message that might well greet us every day with increased meaning. But there is more than today, and the message is not stifled with expansion.

Today was made for you. With love and all good things. But tomorrow you make for yourself. The time of your life is not the moment of today. It lasts many years. Have fun throughout them all.